ETHICS AND THE SOCIAL SCIENCES

ETHICS AND THE SOCIAL SCIENCES

EDITED BY LEO R. WARD, C.S.C.

UNIVERSITY OF NOTRE DAME PRESS · 1959

© 1959

UNIVERSITY OF NOTRE DAME PRESS

NOTRE DAME, INDIANA

CONTRIBUTORS

FRANCIS G. WILSON
Professor of Political Science
University of Illinois

KENNETH E. BOULDING
Professor of Economics
University of Michigan

CHRISTOPHER DAWSON
English historian and sociologist
at present occupying
the chair of Roman Catholic Studies
Harvard University

DAVID BIDNEY
Professor of Anthropology and of Ethics
Indiana University

HERBERT JOHNSTON
Professor of Philosophy
University of Notre Dame

JAMES R. BROWN
Professor of Political Science
Marquette University

Preface

One of the major problems in college and university life now is to bring learning together and to bring learned men together from several and even from many fields. This in part is what these studies by men competent in the social sciences and in ethics have attempted to do.

In times past, some great philosophers have learned from other studies, and have not been in the least ashamed of doing so. Was their philosophy hurt or handicapped by the process? The men in question would never have thought so. One famous philosopher was also a famous biologist, another famous philosopher was a famous theologian, another, and a quite influential one, made remarkable discoveries in mathematics. Specialisms are good, but we are stultified if we cannot learn anything across party lines.

Another good reason for trying to bring ethics and social sciences together, even if only for a moment, is that each needs the other. A mere positivistic social science, say in legal studies and political and economic studies, is quite helpful, but to be able to throw in its full nickel's worth it needs the help of ethics. At least most really aware persons today would say that a political science, standing by itself, and left denuded of ethics, would be little good to the solutions of the world's big and deep problems. Ethics also needs the enrichment of various social sciences, such as history, psychology, and anthropology. Just in our decade, the anthropologist has become aware, and ever so much more circumspectly than the anthropologist of 1880 or of 1920, that moral data, so richly showered on him, must keep asking philosophical questions.

One of the standing difficulties, of course, is to find people who know philosophy and at the same time know any social science, or to find social scientists who have at least some acquaintance with philosophical problems, even with those sticking out of the materials of their own social sciences. Happily, for these conferences, held at the University of Notre Dame in the fall of 1957, we did find competent co-workers in ethics and the social sciences, and we at the University are deeply grateful to the accomplished scholars who for two pleasant days were meeting some of the theoretic and the practical problems arising from the conjunction of ethics and the social sciences.

Naturally, it is difficult to bring the thought of several or many persons to a fine point of unity. In the present effort, an initial advantage was that each of the participants had long been working on both ethical and social problems and each of them had been for some years continuously concerned with the interrelations of ethics and the social sciences. Professor Wilson has long kept close account of our social scientists' assumed or overt affirmation of values and has studied those scientists' implied philosophies and ideologies. Professor Boulding too is well known both as an economist and as a student of the ethical theory involved in economic theory and economic practice, and in recent years he has done a remarkable study, *The Image,* in which he begins with biology and then goes on to psychology and attempts to sketch the conceptual framework of the organism and of organizations and also to bring together under the heading of "the image" their norms and orderings of values. Best known of the contributors was Christopher Dawson who, although unable to be present, was so generous as to do for the conference a brief paper on some relations of ethics and culture. Well known to all who have been following either ethical or anthropological theory is the stand vigorously set forth by Professor Bidney who, well equipped in both anthropology and in Aristotle's ethics, in the present study further refines his position on "relative" and "absolute." Professor Johnston, too, has been working for some years on the interrelations of ethics and the social sciences and in the present paper he has stated with extreme care his understanding of a framework for putting the two together on the basis of Aristotle's distinction of learning into theoretic and practical. Professor James Brown, former director of the special institute at Wesleyan University for studying the effects of theological and moral doctrines on political practice, here brings many matters concretely to a head in a review of some studies and findings by that thriving institute.

LEO R. WARD

Contents

ETHICS AND THE SOCIAL SCIENCES

Chapter I

The Social Scientist and His Values

BY FRANCIS G. WILSON

I

For some time it has been apparent that taxonomic studies of
intellectuals and the values they hold would throw light on both
intellectuals and the nature of contemporary society. The purposes
of this inquiry are, first, to offer some definitions and descriptions
of the intellectuals as a group or a class; and, second, to suggest
a plan of classifying intellectuals by the system of values or social
theories they hold. Value systems are, indeed, the root and the
meaning of the history of intellectuals, or, to say it in more imper-
sonal terms, of intellectual history. The whole essay will be governed by what is conceived to be, in rather general terms, a Thomistic theory of state and society. We may profit by a sociology
of the intellectuals, just as we have gained by social inquiries into
nearly all of the groups in modern society. There is, no doubt,
some resentment against a general inquiry about intellectuals, for
the intellectuals, especially those who are devoted to scientific work,
seem to believe they can stand in judgment on all others.[1] Such
endeavors have reflected the controversies within intellectual life,
as well as the functional exclusiveness or separateness of the intellectual from other members of society.[2] At a somewhat vulgar

1. See my article, "Public Opinion and the Intellectuals," *The American
Political Science Review*, XLVIII (June, 1954), 321.
2. Josef Pieper has observed that there is an exclusiveness among the learned
which is an expression of their difference from the many. But this separateness
or exclusiveness is not an attitude toward the many, or it should not be; and
such exclusiveness does not give rise to a difference in social class. See "On
the Idea of the 'Academic,' " *Thought*, XXX (Winter, 1955-56), 593-594.

1

level, it has resulted at times in the amateur psychoanalysis of the opposition, culminating in the charge that conservatives are a little psychoneurotic because of a concern over "status." In addition, it is suggested, often by implication, that those who are religious are inclined to be authoritarian in their personalities.[3] A sociology of the intellectuals would submit the *libertas philosophandi* to the criticism to which any and all social groups are subject.[4] Such a "process" suggests that as much intellectual activity arises from a metaphysical position as from the traumas resting uneasily in the subconscious. It suggests even that the scientific principle in human relations is the expression of a metaphysical choice. *Quis custodiet custodes?* is always a good question. Who are to judge the intellectuals? Are they above the judgments made by the vulgar, or by individuals outside of the groups of specialized function? Intellectual life has at any moment both the element of metaphysical choice and the fact of function in society.

R. H. S. Crossman has held that the educated elite must subject any conclusions it reaches to the acid test of inexpert common sense, as represented first by the elected politicians, to whom they are responsible between elections, and then by the masses, when they assert their sovereignty at the polls. Crossman insisted at the Milan Cultural Freedom Congress that political wisdom has very little to do with formal education and that character is more important than either knowledge or quickness of wit. He further concluded that the quality of political discussion does not noticeably improve as one ascends from the masses to the experts. Just because a man may know more, he is not necessarily wiser.[5] Both the intellectuals of the right and of the left may have, and often do have, a warm feeling and sympathy with the ordinary mind. Woodrow Wilson

3. See Richard Hofstadter, "The Pseudo-Conservative Revolt," *The American Scholar*, 24 (Winter, 1954-1955), 9 ff. See in general Hofstadter, *The American Political Tradition and the Men Who Made It*, Knopf, 1948, Ch. X, on "Woodrow Wilson: The Conservative as Liberal." The most influential contemporary work treating intellectual positions in the light of Freudian analysis is, of course, T. W. Adorno and Others, *The Authoritarian Personality*, Harper, 1950.

4. Robert B. Sutton, "The Phrase *Libertas Philosophandi*," *Journal of the History of Ideas*, XIV (April, 1953), 310-316.

5. See *The New Leader*, May 7, 1956, Section Two, p. S13. This section is a report of the Milan Cultural Freedom Congress. Harter and Sullivan have suggested that the intellectuals provide the brains for both the defense of the

liked Walter Bagehot and Bagehot liked Shakespeare because he had "a broad tolerance and sympathy for illogical and common minds," and because he had a great ability to understand inferior minds. Bagehot, a sober conservative, had a strong love of the common man with his ordinary opinions. Like Burke, both Bagehot and Wilson saw the common judgment as the cement of society. And at least Bagehot and Burke might agree that only dull nations like the Romans and the British could remain self-governing.[6]

II

It is clear that the formation of values comes through traditions in teaching, in which the intellectuals are the more powerful force. What is meant by intellectuals? When Russell Kirk edited the first number of his new conservative review, *Modern Age,* he said of Julien Benda, "By *clercs,* Benda meant those persons of learning and taste, particularly writers and teachers, whose duty in every age it is to preserve the integrity of moral ideals. They may or may not be clerics; they may or may not be professors; but, if true to their calling, they always are guardians of the Truth. In Benda's eyes, the Truth is the Hellenic view of man and nature."[7] The modern use of the term "intellectual" seems to have emerged in the time of the Dreyfus matter, when the artists and scholars in a sudden political articulateness rallied to his defense. No doubt at the same time they sensed alienation from the dominant bourgeois life of the French nation. The intellectuals demanded justice, and

ruling class and for the revolution. "Though these people, being human, indulge in a lot of self-deception and wishful thinking, their attitudes spring from consideration of ideologies, social movements, history, science, and logic. Whether or not their attitudes or opinions are sound is a delicate matter of value judgments." D. Lincoln Harter and John Sullivan, *Propaganda Handbook,* Twentieth Century Publishing Company, 1953, p. 139.

6. Woodrow Wilson, *Mere Literature and Other Essays,* Houghton Mifflin, 1896, 83 ff.

7. See Russell Kirk, "The Treason of the Clerks," *Modern Age,* I (Summer, 1957), 97. This was a review of Robert J. Neiss, *Julien Benda.* On education and the classical view of man, see H. I. Marrou, *Histoire de l'Éducation dans l'Antiquité,* Éditions du Seuil, 2nd éd., 1950, pp. 297 ff. and *passim.* Marrou noted that the humanistic values in classical education have served the Greek state, Roman civilization, and God since the rise of Christianity.

they were intellectuals in the classical sense, but they were also serving in society in given ways, and they were performing a function in the order of politics.

Such a functional view has been characteristic of much of Continental left-wing discussion of the intellectuals, and, indeed, of the social group, the "intelligentsia." In 1957 Alfred Kantorowicz fled from East to West Germany and denounced the Communist regime as one in which a "wave of terror" was directed against the intellectuals. There has been in East Germany "lawlessness, exploitation of the workers, mental enslavement of the intelligentsia, tyranny by a clique of discredited people who disgrace the conception of socialism. . . ." [8] When Mao-Tse-Tung gave his now noted speech on February 27, 1957, which included the Chinese aphorism, "Let a hundred flowers bloom; let a hundred schools of thought contend," he considered the problem of contradictions among the intellectuals. Diversity was permitted for the development of the arts, science, and a socialist culture. China needed intellectuals for the mighty tasks of socialist construction, but it was obvious that Mao used "intellectual" in a very wide sense to include all educated people who are not capitalists. It covered writers and journalists, university and school teachers, scientists, doctors, and engineers. In Soviet classification, intellectual has, in truth, come to include all who are not peasants and manual workers, thus giving the label of intellectual most surely to the civil servant.[9]

We may say, broadly, that on the Continent the "intellectuals" are generally regarded as functional groups, and a judgment of the quality of the mental operations of an individual is not necessarily included. In America there is something of both definitions, though apparently in recent years an effort to formulate the code of a self-conscious functional intelligentsia has been made. Of course, if the intellectual is defined simply as a functioning person, a person with some peculiar technical or verbal skill, then the quality of the mind is not part of the definition of that person as an intellectual. To

8. See *The Bulletin* (West Germany), August 27, 1957.

9. See supplement to the *New Leader*, September 9, 1957, p. 39, for the comment by G. F. Hudson of Oxford University. Also, Milovan Djilas, *The New Class: An Analysis of the Communist System*, Praeger, 1957: the new class is the class of oligarchs and bureaucrats who have seized a monopoly of power in the Communist state.

define the intellectual in terms of the "rightness" or "oughtness" of his mental operations implies a philosophical foundation for a conception of the intellectual. Milton M. Gordon, in contrast, has defined the intellectual as a person who has a serious and relatively informed interest in ideas and the arts.[10] Unhappily, he seems to omit the person who has scientific knowledge and technical capacity in its application.

There seems to be, however, an effort in the United States to define an intellectual as a "liberal," which might be shown from the American contributions to the recent Milan Cultural Freedom Congress, or in some of the explorations of academic freedom during the past generation.[11] These current controversies over academic freedom, and by implication the role of the intellectual in contemporary society, have grown in large measure out of the attack on the right of Congress to inquire into the Communist affiliation of professors, government employees, journalists, artists, theatrical performers, and lawyers. Peter Viereck has argued that the defense of Senator Joseph R. McCarthy was grounded in old-fashioned populism and progressivism, which has long carried within it a characteristic mistrust of the intellectuals.[12]

But in the very definition of the intellectual as a liberal, that is, in terms of the value formation he represents, there is a judgment of how "intellectual" he is. To attack some persons who are intellectuals is not to attack intelligence, reason, or all intellectuals. Unfortunately, any attack on *some* intellectuals is considered an attack on intelligence. If one defends value against those who base judgment on either fact or instinct, then the value of knowledge is being defended, and *a fortiori* science itself. Such an attack is certainly not "anti-intellectualism" in a proper sense of this much abused

10. See his "Social Class and American Intellectuals," A.A.U.P. *Bulletin,* 40 (Winter, 1954-55), 518.
11. The files of the *Bulletin* of the American Association of University Professors would contain much of the best literature on this problem, though there is a distinguished bibliography in book form on this subject. A book like Morris R. Cohen, *American Thought; A Critical Survey,* The Free Press, 1954, *supports* this idea, at least in the selection of materials.
12. Peter Viereck, "The New American Right," *Arizona Quarterly,* 12 (Autumn, 1956), 197 ff. He comments on what is called the "status-resentment" thesis about the motivation of conservatives, included in Daniel Bell (editor), *The New American Right,* Criterion Books, 1955; Richard Hofstadter's Freudian interpretation of the conservatives also appears in this volume.

word. A critic or intellectual, for example, may be praised for resisting the anti-intellectualist trap, and at the same time such a person may say in the construction of his normative political theory that all religion is pernicious superstition, that sex life should be based directly on a sort of human process of natural selection, that political movements are absurd, and that all of the recent wars, say against the Nazis and the Communists, are lacking in any rational determination of justice or injustice. In not infrequent instances, the term anti-intellectual is simply a pejorative term for theological inquiry, and philosophy that is not pragmatic or empirical in its epistemology, or even efforts to demonstrate the reasonableness of humanistic values. One may be opposed to some intellectuals simply because one is in favor of using intelligence in attacking social and political questions.[13]

In most situations, the quality of mind and the functional skills within a given "public" become involved. By intellectuals we may thus mean, among others, teachers at nearly all levels and in all kinds of institutions; writers, journalistic and otherwise; the practitioners and critics of the arts; scientific and technical people, such as financial experts, doctors, lawyers, engineers and the vast staffs of scientific and research institutions; management in industry; and civil servants in the higher professional brackets.

Now in every such group of intellectuals there are methods of expressing the common interest. Language here is the vocabulary or the "jargon" of the skill, and the ideas accepted by the intellectuals concerned.[14] Among all intellectuals there is a traditional and accepted rhetoric that is used to discipline the group internally and to defend its interests against outside critics. Often such modes of expression are not suitable for communication with just anyone; in this case the common and general language of controversy must

13. Consult C. S. Lewis, *The Abolition of Man,* Macmillan, 1946, pp. 21 ff., for a brilliant discussion of the doctrine of Objective Value, including the Chinese idea of *Tao* and the Western principle of natural law.

14. Jargon applied to contemporary social science suggests the unnecessary invention of technical words, often Latinate in origin, but which do not carry a precise enough meaning to advance in reality "scientific" discourse. Or, as Webster's Unabridged Dictionary suggests, it is "The technical, esoteric, or secret vocabulary of a science, art, trade, sect, profession, or other special group. . . ."

be used.[15] Intellectuals become marked as groups largely because of traditions in learning, religion, judgment, and philosophy. A social scientist who is a Catholic becomes conscious early in his career of profound differences in the traditions within his discipline, and particularly in social sciences other than his own. He becomes aware that the roots of a value system, which is being both preserved and reformed by teaching, constitute the chief problem of intellectual history. Ideas are weapons, intellectual history is a weapon, and value systems are the weapons of those who teach. In this sense, the study of the formation of values is the reason in intellectual history.

III

The more important proposition to begin with is that a discrimination between value systems leads easily and properly into a classification of intellectuals. It is more meaningful than trying to place them in a scale of the "middle class." [16] If one is at all committed in the intellectual sieges of the present, a sense of difference in quality and kind of intellectual is certain to arise. And for a Scholastic thinker who stands inevitably somewhere outside the postulates of positivistic liberalism, a knowledge of conflict rewards one with a deeper perspective, a further dimension of understanding, than the contestant living merely within some secular system can have. While the secular mind has attempted to ignore Christian thought, and more particularly Catholic thought, for the Thomistic thinker it is simply impossible to be unconcerned with those

15. Mortimer J. Adler has said that "with exceptions so rare that even they may be doubted, philosophers do not actually join issue. Philosophers fail to disagree because they fail to achieve the minimal topical agreements prerequisite to genuine disagreement." Adler believes that the next significant advance in philosophy will come from a developed art of constructing philosophical controversies, in which the issue between individuals will be understood and will be joined. See Adler, "Controversy in the Life and Teaching of Philosophy," *Proceedings* of the American Catholic Philosophical Association, XXX (April, 1956), 19, 16-35.

16. Milton M. Gordon, "Social Class and American Intellectuals, A.A.U.P. *Bulletin,* Winter, 1954-55, p. 524: ". . . the most plausible hypothesis is that the basic social status position from which the intellectual looks out on the American scene is that of the upper middle class. Intellectuals below this level are drawn upward to it by aspiration, intellectuals above it are drawn down by participation."

with whom one is inevitably in conflict. A Thomist, thus, will know more about both Catholics and liberals, than the traditional liberal will know about Catholics.

Intellectual history is often a kind of taxonomic effort that charts the evolution of intellectual elites. It offers a history of the philosophic, professional, and learned types who have attained sovereignty in particular centers of intellectual work, such as the historically famous universities and national capitals. One thinks readily of Italian university towns, or of the University of Paris through a long and changing history. The type of person in power illustrates a change in the kind of intellectuality that has been respectable, or, the kind of metaphysical choices that such an elite makes. In some instances the differences have been chiefly in modes or styles of expression. Modern social scientists, for example, seek to attain a technicality, distinctness, and objectivity in expression that fulfills at least the literary requirements of scientific method.[17] While there have been many significant changes in style in Catholic intellectual life, they have been more deliberate and less experimental than among other intellectuals.[18] Here again is one of the reasons for the sense of perspective that the Catholic intellectual

17. Edward L. Bernays, for example, has assumed the general social applicability of much of the findings of contemporary social science. In *Public Relations*, Oklahoma University Press, 1952, 215, he has urged that those engaged in salesmanship should use the new knowledge of man being developed by America's thirty thousand social scientists, and thus gain entrance to the hidden markets of the human personality.

Obviously, such a problem involves finally questions of academic freedom, freedom notably to differ from the orthodoxy of a given discipline, or "state of the science." See Russell Kirk, *Academic Freedom; An Essay in Definition,* Regnery, 1955, pp. 135, 136: "Now I think that what the doctrinaire liberals— more properly called disintegrated liberals, perhaps—like Mr. Commager, Mr. Taylor and Mr. Hutchins fear is really, in their heart of hearts, themselves. Their neat little world of Progress and Civil Liberties Committees and Welfare Legislation and Goodness of Humankind has dissolved, overnight, into its constituent atoms. . . . The reader may have gathered that I do not much respect the present opinions of doctrinaire liberals on the subject of academic freedom." Note Richard Hofstadter and Walter P. Metzger, *The Development of Academic Freedom in the United States,* Columbia University Press, 1955. Also Journet Kahn, "The Threat To Academic Freedom," *Proceedings,* American Catholic Philosophical Association, 1956, p. 160 ff.

18. See for example, the conclusions that may be drawn from a Thomistic history of philosophy. F. J. Thonnard, *A Short History of Philosophy,* trans. by E. A. Marziarz, Declée (N. Y.), 1955. There is both continuity and change in the deliberate moderation of philosophical style.

may have in relation to his critical fellow citizens in the City of Learning.

IV

Now the social sciences form a group of disciplines in the contemporary university. As university disciplines, the social sciences are young; they are still a little like budgetary and curricular experiments. Political science, for example, can be considered either very old, as it is assumed to be in the study of the history of political thought, or it may be considered to be exceedingly young, not being introduced into American university studies until late in the last century. It can be regarded as either an off-shoot of history or of political economy. It may be considered the lineal descendant of Aristotle's *Politics* and the brilliant Greek inquiry into government. But in relation to the value systems of a society, the social sciences are not new, and the interpretative mechanisms of all of the social sciences are correlated with the methodolgy that is popular at a given time. Logical method, mathematical systems, such as geometry in the seventeenth century, history, biology, the analogy of physics, and the modern formulation of a "scientific method," have all influenced the study of society. But the concern for method, especially a quantitative, empirical and value-skeptical method, is predominant in the social sciences in our time.

On the other hand, the social scientists must make their metaphysical choices in the larger contexts of life, just as all other intellectuals must. In each instance, the social sciences extend from inconsequential and small jobs of calculation, enumeration, or classification, to the abstract ideas one may find in the most significant of the political philosophers. In some of the social sciences there is a greater unity of method, postulates, and subject-matter than in others. Sociology, for example, is more monolithic in what is respectable method and postulate than political science; and economics falls closer to political science than to anthropology and psychology. A political scientist, thus, has more freedom than a sociologist both in the formulation of his value system and in the expression of it. In other words, one may say that some social sciences have more "jargon" than others, and some resort more to the

Latinate vocabulary than others. But whatever one may say, the social sciences are struggling desperately to be sciences, to have a share in the training of public servants and in the formulation of good and evil entail. Indeed, it has been said that many intellectuals are not anti-Communist because scholarly detachment is not compatible with believing in evil, the evil of people or the evil of movements such as communism. Richard Weaver has suggested that such intellectuals must continue to dance in the excluded middle.[19]

One thing is certain: the Thomistic social scientist becomes conscious of the different sets of presuppositions used by his brethren. He must make a choice of allies within his discipline. And he must make this choice in the light of an already accomplished formation of values, and in the light of a formation of judgment that is constantly in process. With a Catholic perspective, the social scientist can see readily the newer trends in subject-matter and method, for methods of inquiry are often used to discriminate between philosophical positions. It has been proposed that the foundations, notably the Ford Foundation, allocate a large sum to subsidize the publication of works in the social sciences. It is almost certain that such a sum would be spent largely in the light of "doctrine" and the experimental testing of the proper methodolgy for social science. Such a program would not, in the condition of the universities today, be neutral between the metaphysical positions that are actually taken in the secular academic world in the social sciences. Intellectuals who might control such funds would have an enormous power; a power which would operate as a lever toward conformity in the subject-matter and method acceptable and respectable in professional life. It might eventually operate as a kind of monopoly power in the formation of the minds and spirits of whole classes of university intellectuals.[20]

19. See in general Richard M. Weaver, *The Ethics of Rhetoric,* Chicago University Press, 1953. With every episode like the invasion of Finland, the Nazi-Russian pact, the war in Korea, and the suppression of revolts in Eastern Europe, notably Hungary, a number of intellectuals leave the Communist parties, as well as fellow travellers who publicly repent.

20. On group conformism in America in general, including the intellectuals, see William H. Whyte, *The Organization Man,* Simon and Shuster, 1956. See especially Chapter 18.

V

A central purpose of this essay is to offer a preliminary classification of intellectual groups through the values a Catholic social scientist must live with as a member of his particular profession. The shading of intellectual positions on values is so complicated that no brief statement can be complete. However, the larger and more precise positions may be sketched, and other values can be grouped with these in such a way that the meaning is not distorted. Moreover, the values within a given profession, as they relate to the dialectic between the Thomist and the non-Thomist, are not exclusive to that group. Value systems run through modern life, and they clearly run through different social sciences. But there are changing emphases, and a social scientist of one discipline will not state a proposition in the same manner as the member of another. A political scientist will not speak the same way as an anthropologist, and the anthropologist will not speak as the economist, though the anthropologist and sociologist will come closer together than some of the others. Nor will the proposition involved be held at the same level of importance or intensity in two different social sciences.[21]

Three classes of social scientists may be observed. (A) There are those who consider values as nothing more than the subjective commitment of an individual. These social scientists are generally concerned with newer developments in the theory and practice of method. (B) There are those who are indifferent to values, or who think of them as very simple incidents in the examination of social and moral issues. (C) Finally, there are those who do not consider values to be subjective, and who will admit that acceptable ones are subject to rational proof. Implicitly, then, some order of rational judgment about values is possible.

(A) Let us consider the first class, or those who believe values

21. No extraordinary claims for classification are made. The author is impressed with Eric Voegelin, *Order and History,* Vol. I, *Israel and Revelation,* Louisiana State University Press, 1956, pp. 62-63: "The intelligible order of history cannot be found through classification of phenomena; it must be sought through a theoretical analysis of institutions and experiences of order, as well as the form that results from their interpretation." We must reach above the level of construction of empirical types.

are subjective preferences, or commitments of the will. To begin with, two subclasses may be observed. (a) The first group is pre-occupied with empirical study in the social sciences, the behavioral sciences, or the policy sciences. Notable sums have been given by the Ford Foundation to advance behavioral study, and some highly-publicized occurrences have taken place, such as the jury wire-tapping case, in which the deliberations of a jury were recorded without the jurymen being aware of it. Indeed, attempts seem to be made to change the general name of the social sciences to the "social and behavioral sciences." At least this is the reference of the volume of *American Men of Science* that has been in preparation for the social sciences. Many believe that the new and broader development of the social and policy sciences is to take place precisely in the area of the study of behavior. Thomism comes in conflict with the empiricist when more is claimed for behavioral methods than can logically be asserted, or when it is claimed that scientific methods show there is no system of proof beyond the empirical and the quantitative. The denial of values becomes often quite as intuitive as the assertion of them. The denial of the rational proof of value which comes within behavioral methods must, in truth, be a matter of proof, as much as any other aspect of social study. Formally, the behavioral intellectuals profess an indifference to religion and to theistically inspired values. But in fact there is no neutrality, for religious values are not considered subject to proof in their theory of method, which is in fact a theory of proof. We have been reminded that they labor at the "frontier of research," and at times they may speak of the revolution of the behavioral sciences as having already occurred. Game theory, for example, is one of the fields of investigation, just as the recent studies of "the authoritarian personality." [22]

22. See Stephen K. Bailey and Others, *Research Frontiers in Politics and Government,* Brookings Institution, 1955. It has been suggested that the consensus of the Milan Congress was that there is no longer any need for an explicit system of beliefs, and it is futile to distinguish between socialism and free-enterprise. See *Encounter,* November, 1955. Cited by Frank S. Meyer, "Politics and Responsibility," *National Review,* April 4, 1955, p. 21. Professor John P. Roche has said, in disparagement of principle: "Every society, sociological research suggests, has its set of myths which incorporate and symbolize its political, economic and social aspirations. Thus, as medieval society has the Quest for the Holy Grail and the cult of numerology. . . ," we have in our time the dream of impartial decision-making. What objectivity in this case

The type of social scientist just discussed is becoming more and more prominent and powerful in both the universities and the foundations. Never before has so much foundation money been available for distribution to those who accept the current orthodoxy in method and in political position.[23] Obviously a Christian philosopher is not opposed to empirical and behavioral study in social relations, or more particularly in politics and sociology. But a Thomist is bound to be critical of some forms of empiricism, or of a position which denies or minimizes the possibility of philosophical proof. He will say that a man rebels at being nothing more than a social animal; in the midst of the Freudian "darkness" he would retain the image of charity in man. However, the pervasive development of "group research" and the vast sums that are available to those who engage in the proper kind of research may be on the point of remaking the whole university structure of the social sciences. There is some encouraging development in Catholic social study, but it often seems to be living in separation and isolation. Method, in other words, is often a sectarian weapon. In the behavioral sciences philosophy seems at times to be held as nothing, and as Parain has said the fact has been deified in order to humiliate the thought.[24]

Of late there has been a remarkable extension of Freudian ideas

might amount to, under the impetus of behavioral method, is that the Constitution, for example, could become what social scientists say the majority consensus is. See Roche, "Judicial Self-Restraint," *The American Political Science Review,* XLIX (September, 1955), 762.

23. In the 83rd Congress, 1954, the Reece Committee, the Special Committee to Investigate Tax-Exempt Foundations, created an enormous stir, and extended statements in defense of tax-exemption were offered, among others, by the Rockefeller Foundation and the General Education Board. The Ford Foundation, and its Fund for the Republic, became a central issue because of the doctrinal positions and the political activity of the Fund. It is fairly obvious that tax-exemption, plus philosophical and political positions, pose a long-run problem.

24. Brice Parain, "Against the Spirit of Neutrality," *Confluence,* 4 (January, 1956), 380-381, but see pp. 359 ff. Parain says (p. 387): "We are paid scholars on reprieve for deserting; let us carry on our profession as students. One thing we do know, and that is that our people are in despair. They sense that they are getting nowhere. . . . All they hear is nonsense." Albert Moraczewski, O.P., "The Contribution of Science to Religion," *Bulletin of the Atomic Scientists,* XIII (January, 1957), 31: ". . . It would be well to observe that both science and religion have a growing core of established, permanent truths. These are not, and can never be in conflict. Surrounding this core is a penumbra of doctrines, facts, and theories in various stages of proof."

to the study of the whole personality, with correlative applications to public policy. The person is viewed as a psychological whole, as a system of syndromes, of clustering ideas and evaluations of people and situations. On the one hand, the restriction of absolute majoritarianism by some form of natural right is repudiated in the defense of the majority; but, on the other hand, the majority is contemned by others who resort to Freudian or Freudian-related explanations of behavior. Frank S. Meyer has reminded us: "It is the triumphant production of a deep-psychological explanation for the obvious which gives one the sensation of dealing with the victims of a mass delusion as one reads the papers of the 'psychoanalytically oriented' social scientists. . . . Every sign of individualist or traditional resistance to the tyranny of contemporary conformity is attributed to the authoritarian personality." [25] One is tempted to use Freudian concepts to explain anti-Thomist value systems, but the Thomist is committed to philosophical or rational discussion.[26]

(b) The second subclass may or may not be concerned with the current methodological inquiry. Here, the social scientist is informed by hostility toward religious values, considering them to be mere superstitions, or dangerous barriers to rational social behavior.[27] While a social scientist in this category is formally a defender

25. See Frank S. Meyer, "Symptoms of Mass Delusion," *National Review*, February 8, 1956, p. 23. See, of course, T. W. Adorno and Others, *The Authoritarian Personality*. The literature that has been inspired by this volume is truly remarkable. It is not only difficult to get the book out of a university library, but it is also unlikely that one can avoid being subjected to at least part of the "F" or Fascism scale, the "Berkeley F Scale."

26. On one occasion Peter Viereck said that anti-Catholicism is the anti-Semitism of the intellectuals. See Iago Galdston, M.D., "Psychopathic Intellectuals," *The Pacific Spectator*, X (Spring, 1956), 100-101. Galdston not only psychoanalyzes the intellectuals in the usual libidinous terms, but he also suggests the pattern of mental response. For example, "the intellectual—*qua* egghead—is an enthusiastic planner, an unconscionable manipulator of man, society, and the universe, and a gullible sucker for everything that carries the label of science. . . . The intellectual's framework of operations is a derivative of the intellectual bias developed in and by eighteenth-century science." Galdston's criticism is not anti-intellectual, in his view; rather, it is pro-intelligence.

27. Robert E. Lane, in describing the authoritarian syndrome, says that one characteristic of this personality is a "tendency to accept superstitious or supernatural explanations and to avoid scientific explanations." He may be slightly more extreme in his judgment than the original work on the authoritarian personality; but this might be a matter of argument. See Lane, "Political Personality and Electoral Choice," *The American Political Science Review*, XLIV (March, 1955), 176.

of liberty, such as civil liberty and academic freedom, as defined in current public controversy, there is always a point where he will decide that suppression, censorship, and counter-propaganda through the control of the media of mass communication is proper and legitimate. The comic-strip mind may have no rights, but the defender of the general welfare may not restrict comic books.[28] While these situations are commonly recognized and applied during war, the issue here is the application of such ideas in normal times. Furthermore, the extension of Freudian ideas to politics has produced what may be properly called a Freudian theory of liberal suppression. The point is simply this: the authoritarian personality is not suited to the democratic process, and the government is justified in restricting, controlling, and directing such personalities in the share they may have in the course of democratic politics. The authors of *The Authoritarian Personality* say, in what is probably the most important and revealing passage in the work: "In our present-day struggle to achieve a strengthening of the tolerant, liberal point of view we may have to avoid presenting the prejudiced individual with more ambiguities than he is able to absorb and offer instead, in some spheres at least, solutions which are constructive. . . . Efforts to modify the 'prejudiced' pattern may have to make use of authorities — though by no means necessarily of authoritarian authorities — in order to reach the individual in question. This follows from the fact that it is authority more than anything else that structures or prestructures the world of the prejudiced individual. Where public opinion takes over the function of authority and provides the necessary limitations — and thus certainties — in many walks of daily life, as is the case in this country, there will be some room for the tolerance of national or racial ambiguities. It must be emphasized, however, that the potentially beneficial aspects of conformity are more than counterbalanced by the inherent seeds of stereotype and prejudgment. These latter trends are apt to increase in a culture which has become too complex to be fully mastered by the individual."[29]

28. Cf. John Courtney Murray, S.J., "Literature and Censorship," *Books on Trial,* June-July, 1956, pp. 1 ff.
29. Adorno, *op. cit.,* 486. Bernard Berelson, in his discussion of the application of quantitative studies of public opinion to the theory of democracy, has suggested that the authoritarian personality is unsuited to the democratic

In the minds of many social scientists both suppression and control may be used against persons who are considered to have ideas that are superstitious, who are ignorant, prejudiced, insane or who are like maniacs influencing the ignorant, who suffer from other forms of mental ill-health, who are irresponsible or demagogic in public discussion, who show sympathy for the Fascist forms of subversion and conspiracy, who would restrict the right of the scientific professions to determine public policy, or who, finally, would retard "adjustment" to the American way of life. A little reflection will show there are numerous ways in which individuals holding such ideas or exhibiting such behavior may be dealt with, even within the customary pattern of democratic politics. Since to such intellectuals the historical and Western religions, except the most diluted forms of deism and ethicism, are disvalues, these individuals are particularly hostile to Catholic views on the natural law, marriage, and the teaching authority of the Church. On these issues it will be insisted that Protestants, though basically as unrealistic as Catholics, are less dangerous to the march of progress. The criticisms of Catholic positions fall into a modernized, streamlined, and urbane form of free-thinking, but such thinking has, of course, been characteristic of liberalism from Condorcet, for example, through John Dewey.[30]

(B) The second large class is essentially value-indifferent, but values are accepted to some degree at least. The point here, however, is that social and moral ideas are simple questions, and they are hardly worth discussion. Technical men, such as engineers and social scientists whose minds are formed in an analogous manner, are often in this category. The technical man is, thus, in mental process, like the social scientist who is concerned almost exclusively with the description and charting of his subject-matter. There is little interpretation of social process, or of social purpose, and little

---

process. He is not clear whether he would support some device that would exclude such people from the various forms of political participation. Democratic theorists have indicated, by implication in any case, that participation in a democratic life is a therapeutic agent which would be lost if the proposals of Adorno and Others were implemented. See Berelson, "Democratic Theory and Public Opinion," *The Public Opinion Quarterly,* XVI (Fall, 1952), 313 ff.

30. See my article, "What is a Conservative American Economy?" *Current Economic Comment,* 18 (February, 1956), 23.

sense of the possible meaning of events as history. At times there is a stubborn reluctance to engage in any evaluative discussion, partly one assumes because of a lack of knowledge or skill in philosophical discourse. When values become simple problems, the reasons adduced in their support are often contradictory and disordered. Yet, in contrast there are individuals who think they know much more than they really do about philosophy and theology. Such a condition is not unusual with all of us perhaps, but is peculiarly acute with the social scientist whose thinking is technical and descriptive.

(a) The primary subclass seems to be characterized by a sort of jelly-fish religious affiliation. These intellectuals may go to church, but they hardly seem to have any doctrines. They are quite indifferent about the existence or non-existence of the supernatural, and those with a firm belief are considered to be objects of mild amusement. Subclass two (b) seems to be in general composed of scientific intellectuals who do not know or do not care about philosophical inquiry, but who nevertheless are likely to be deterministic in social and moral theory, explaining human behavior by curiously simple conceptions of motivation drawn from economics and psychology. Adhering to either an economic or psychological view of life, moral issues are subordinated and without importance. In spite of ineptitude in social knowledge, scientists are at times notably vocal on political issues rather remote from public policy dealing with their own areas of specialization.

(C) The first group of social scientists overlaps, of course, with a third group who in some form admit there is a philosophical proof of values. Those we have already discussed would admit only a purely empiric, statistical, or quantitative proof of values. It would be a behavioral or "scientific" proof and not a philosophical argument. (a) Now, the first subclass in the third class follows the tradition of the French Revolution; these intellectuals are hostile to religion as the Enlightenment was, or as Latin liberalism has been. Positive science is regarded as the only basis for progress.[31] Other

---

31. See the able criticisms of positivism in Eric Voegelin, *The New Science of Politics,* Columbia University Press, 1952, Introduction, 1 ff.: on p. 8: "The use of method as the criterion of science abolishes theoretical advance." All propositions concerning facts become scientific if they are gathered in the proper manner, and in this case all facts tend to be equal. Hallowell has said: "The

than deism, such as reflected in the writings of Montesquieu, for example, religion is unacceptable, and neither poetic intuition nor spiritual insight can be a foundation for social advance. And a choice of values is to be effected through the instruction of pragmatism, or of some form of neo-utilitarianism. Values are proved in terms of a pragmatic epistemology, by a test of workability that is difficult to define, a theory of the content of science in the relations of men, in terms of a hedonistic calculation of human behavior, or in the light of facts or instincts. We are dealing here with a profoundly wide cleavage in the study of politics in America, for the neo-Scholastic would surely seek for justice, and he would assume the correctness and validity of what Walter Lippmann in 1955 called *The Public Philosophy*. Moreover, he would reject the left-wing materialism of the Marxians. France, the home of the philosophy of the Enlightenment, is torn today by the schism of the soul that is born of the conflicts in philosophy that have stemmed from the eighteenth century. Men who are loyal to a philosophy are sometimes driven to uncertainty in their love for a disordered fatherland.

(b) The second subclass has a recessive religious background; as individuals these intellectuals retain their youthful religious attitudes, though they are primarily concerned to support temporal or political "causes," such as the United Nations, the New Deal, or other humanitarian or reformist movements. Numbers of writers and political leaders of the Progressive Era in the United States might be cited, as well as many holders of academic chairs.[32] Woodrow Wilson is surely of this type, and one whose remarkable career spanned from the graduate school, the professorship, and university presidency to being President of the United States. The

---

inadequacy of positivism. . . is proven in this fact: that the positivist cannot avoid engaging in the metaphysical speculation he claims to have dispensed with." John H. Hallowell, *Main Currents in Modern Political Thought*, Holt, 1950, 321.

32. One may be reminded of the professor before World War I who taught his students there were three essential reforms to bring about the best possible social order: woman's suffrage, prohibition, and a League of Nations. Obviously, many Progressives had to look for new reforms to advocate in the 1920's. Something like this may be used to explain softness toward Communism in the early years after the Russian Revolution.

campaign speeches of 1912, "The New Freedom," may well be cited as evidence of this kind of attitude.[33] Such intellectuals are often friendly, or they try to be so, tolerant, and sometimes even sympathetic toward the Thomist intellectual. A large number of the "traditional" types of social scientists falls into this class. They are concerned with their specializations, without being hostile to the idea that a rational defense of values is possible. Nor would they lean upon the thesis that conservative political and economic attitudes today have no relation to rational ideas, or that they are simply the evidence of a Fascist-like or authoritarian personality structure. Often these intellectuals are not sharply aware of philosophic issues and terminology, but they are convinced that the proper choice of demonstrable values is the heart of any social science. Like Thomist intellectuals, they are often willing to work with intellectuals outside of the university elite. At worst they may simply weep for those who disagree with them, or with those who break over the lines of "doctrine" or respectability, and at best they understand that one tolerates a human being rather than the ideas he may hold.

Subclass three (c) affirms religious values at the foreground of social science, and religious discussion blends readily into philosophical inquiry. Indeed, there are times when the non-Thomistic intellectual may have a greater concern for religious issues at the forefront of politics than is commonly found among Catholic intellectuals. The Thomist perhaps distinguishes more sharply the spiritual and the temporal, and the philosophic finality of the state is grounded more in natural law theory than in purely theological propositions. Here, one often finds the Catholic, Protestant, and Jew united in common human enterprises. Practically all of the intellectuals in this class would view the troubles of the present as a moral crisis. Such intellectuals turn to a moral analysis based on

33. John W. Davidson (editor), *A Crossroads of Freedom; The 1912 Campaign Speeches of Woodrow Wilson,* Yale University Press, 1956. This volume clearly replaces the long traditional compilation of these speeches, *The New Freedom* (1913). Very soon after the election of 1912 there was a loss of interest in reform, which was not revived until the depression and the rise of Fascism in the 1930's. Cf. Arthur S. Link, *Wilson: The New Freedom,* Princeton University Press, 1956, 468-69.

reason or revelation to help resolve, if possible, the questions of the day.[34]

VI

Let us make some observations by way of conclusion. The rivals of the Thomist intellectual are, first, those who hold values are subjective preferences and who are actively hostile to religious beliefs; and, second, those who reject the concept of value as subjective preference but hold to the judgments of the Enlightenment, and more especially to an emergent American version of the anticlericalism of certain European and Latin American countries.

The function of the Thomist intellectual in these circumstances is twofold. He must understand the historical matrix out of which a value arises, and he should use such opportunity as he may have to present the elements of theistic philosophy and the social prudence that is grounded at its beginning in the *philosophia perennis*. Communists often speak of the duty of the party members and workers to maintain contact with the masses. With uncertain success, this is precisely what the liberal intellectuals seek always to do. In some periods it has been peculiarly true of Thomist intellectuals. It was true in the time of the Counter-Reformation; it was a powerful factor in the Catholic revival during the nineteenth century; and we may watch it even today with approval in those areas where the struggle with Communists has been most acute. When some intellectuals say that the people cannot govern, it may mean only that a chasm exists between the self-appointed intelligentsia and the unpretentious man.[35]

Many social scientists are becoming insistent on the right to

---

34. See Hallowell, *op. cit., passim.* One of the most distinguished of contemporary Thomistic thinkers is Jacques Maritain. Of his many books *Man and the State,* Chicago University Press, 1951, is probably the best to cite for this line of thought. See *Social Order,* November, 1955, for discussions of Maritain's ethical theory by Francis J. Marien and Philip S. Land.

35. Did not John Stuart Mill say, in the Introduction to his *On Liberty:* "Despotism is a legitimate mode of government in dealing with barbarians, provided the end be their improvement, and the means justified by actually effecting that end. Liberty, as a principle, has no application to any state of things anterior to the time when mankind have become capable of being improved by free and equal discussion?" But who is to judge whether there exists a state of barbarism?

govern, assuming that social science training, especially in the behavioral sciences, is the proper apprenticeship for membership in the political class.[36] In implication a monopoly of social intelligence is claimed by denying it to others, such as those holding religious beliefs or who are conservatives. Lionel Trilling has said: "In the United States at this time liberalism is not only the dominant but even the sole intellectual tradition. For it is the plain fact that nowadays there are no conservative or reactionary ideas in general circulation. . . . But the conservative impulse and the reactionary impulse do not, with some isolated and some ecclesiastical exceptions, express themselves in ideas but only in action or in irritable mental gestures which seek to resemble ideas."[37] There are, of course, equally sharp replies, and it can begin with the application of Freudian ideas to the critics of the Thomist and his allies. If conservatives have status trouble, as Hofstadter, following *The Authoritarian Personality,* suggests, so may also the liberal intellectuals, particularly the critics and the social scientists who have not been given the recognition in governing that they seem to believe they should have. It has been suggested, indeed, that many of the modern intellectuals all over the world, and particularly in the West, have suffered a kind of trauma, which prevents them from seeing the world and reality as it is, and which drives them to hold philosophies that are contrary to those who actually have a considerable degree of influence. American intellectuals, it is said, are suffering from a trauma, a schism of the soul, a sense of guilt at having made great mistakes in their judgments about history, and their inability to provide for the realization of policy in a disordered world.

The first trauma was, perhaps, a premature sympathy for Bol-

36. Edward Shils, "Freedom and Influence: Observations on the Scientists' Movement in the United States," *Bulletin of the Atomic Scientists,* XIII (January, 1957), 17: "The self-esteem of the intellectuals does not, however, foster academic freedom when it expresses an extreme belief that the only proper regime is that of the 'philosopher king.' The fundamental nature of the free society—a plurality of autonomous spheres bound together by a sense of affinity and the collaboration of equals — is infringed on and harm done to all sides when scientists and scholars esteem themselves to the point where they regard the elite of the political and economic spheres as unworthy, incompetent, and repugnant."
37. *The Liberal Imagination; Essays on Literature and Society,* p. ix.

shevism and the Russian Revolution as a means for uplifting the common man; the second trauma was, perhaps, involvement in the United Front during the 1930's, when in fact Fascism was resisted at the price of assisting Communism; in a third instance, the liberal social scientists affirmed their separation from the masses and probably the majority in resisting the efforts in Congress to expose Communism, as in the campaign against the Dies Committee and its various successors; and, finally, in "breaking" Senator McCarthy there were times when the statement of issues was hardly up to the standard of rational discussion. Milosz has insisted that the alienation from the masses, which many intellectuals sense in anguish, is one of the forces which makes intellectuals turn toward Communism, and in times past toward the totalitarian movements in Germany and Italy.[38] And Diana Trilling has noted that "most anti-Communist liberals have been through the Communist mill, or frighteningly close to it." [39]

Should the new elite, the elite of social science intellectuals, who in the universities, in government, and in the foundations, already have such great power, be successful in their claims, it would be a catastrophe and a disaster for Catholic and Thomist intellectuals. It would not merely exclude them from their inherent rights as citizens to be consulted in a pluralistic society, but it would exclude from the calculations of policy the whole corpus of ideas associated with natural law and Christian morality.[40] All intellectuals, Tho-

38. Czeslaw Milosz, *The Captive Mind,* Knopf, 1953; see also "Murti-Bing," *The Twentieth Century,* July, 1951, p. 12: "The great longing of the 'alienated' intellectual is to belong to the masses. It is such a powerful longing that, in trying to appease it, a great many of them who once looked to Germany or Italy for inspiration have now become converted to the New Faith [communism]." See also Gabriel A. Almond, *The Appeals of Communism,* Princeton University Press, 1954. It is unfortunate that Freudian techniques are used to explain why people become Communists, just as the same techniques are used to explain why one is either a liberal or a conservative. One of the most common uses is to say that the religious conversion of a former Communist, *e.g.,* Whittaker Chambers, simply shows a need to *submit* to authority. Adorno, *op. cit., passim,* considers this desire to submit an evidence of prefascist tendency.
39. *Partisan Review,* May-June, 1950, p. 486. Used by Towner Phelan, St. Louis Union Trust Company *Letter,* January, 1952, No. 59.
40. Morris R. Cohen said in 1954: "It is reasonable to expect that the contributions of American Catholics to Catholic philosophy, which are just beginning, will eventually assume large proportions. All the indications to date make

mist as well as others, want opinions to count, and they are aware that people remote from power can be so tolerant that all ideas become in color like a nondescript gray. In such situations, when there is a loss of taste or form in both ways of living and in moral ideas, people may want little more than the enjoyment of a well-being assured by the state. In the end, it may be assumed that the Thomist intellectual can accept as pluralist democracy neither unrestrained majoritarianism, nor a control of government by social science intellectuals who have only a recessive moral sense. Any intellectual should recognize that by definition he is part of an elite, either by the gifts of a trained intelligence or by the preference of professional duties. He might well remember what Woodrow Wilson said to the Princeton undergraduates on election evening in 1912: "The lesson of this election is a lesson of responsibility . . . I summon you for the rest of your lives to work to set this government forward by processes of justice, equity and fairness." [41]

---

it probable that the contributions of American Catholics to social ethics will be more American than Catholic." *Op. cit.,* p. 188. Clearly, it is easier to distinguish the national adjustment from the universal within the Church than from without.

41. Davidson, *op. cit.,* p. 525. One of the notable publications in this area is Daniel Lerner, Harold D. Lasswell and Others, *The Policy Sciences; Recent Developments in Scope and Method,* Stanford University Press, 1951. Robert K. Merton and Lerner analyze the problem of "Social Scientists and Research Policy," and on p. 292, say: "If he [the social scientist] is to play an effective role in putting his knowledge to work, it is increasingly necessary that he affiliate with a bureaucratic power-structure in business or government." If he affiliates here, he loses his position in academic circles, but if he stays with the academic he usually loses the resources to carry through his research on a significant scale. At one point these authors speak of the "bureaucratic intellectual."

As it stands, the functioning elites in public policy do so without outside criticism or responsibility. But the advocacy of a social science elite, while hesitant, is quite real. Hofstadter has urged an "elite with political and moral autonomy." This is taken from his article in *The American Scholar,* already cited above. But see Bernard Rosenberg, "The New American Right," *Dissent,* III (Winter, 1956), 45-50. Rosenberg notes that Talcott Parsons wants a new American elite, a social strata with a sense of political responsibility. It is not at all clear what will happen to democracy, if democracy means an effective freedom of public opinion to determine public policy. Cf. C. Wright Mills, *The Power Elite,* Oxford University Press, 1956.

Chapter II

The Knowledge of Value
and the Value of Knowledge

BY KENNETH E. BOULDING

I

This paper is essentially an application of parts of the theory
of the Image, as outlined in my book by that title.[1] I should therefore begin by sketching the framework of this basic theory.

What I mean by the "Image" is the *cognitive structure* or "subjective knowledge" possessed by an organism or organization. The
image is seen in its most clear and developed form in man, but the
interpretation of the behavior of all the lower forms of life, even
down to the one-celled organism, involves simpler forms of an
image concept, and the understanding of the behavior of social organizations likewise calls for the concept of a structure of images
in its component organisms. The image, then, is the "view of the
universe" held by an organism. This "view" may be fairly simple
in the case of an amoeba, consisting of little more than a dim
awareness of the distinction between food and not-food, between
a time to eat and a time to divide, or perhaps between danger and
not-danger. In the case of man the image is extremely complex.
It includes elaborate images of time and space, images of the self
and of other persons, images of objects and their properties, images
of predictive laws (what will happen if—), images of language
and skills, and so on. Though confined in the nutshell of his body,
man is indeed king of infinite space; the galaxies and the eons, the

1. *The Image: Knowledge in Life and Society*, University of Michigan Press,
1956.

25

round world and all that therein is, the triumph and tragedy of the human heart, are all within him as well as outside him, portrayed on the enormous many-dimensioned screen of his image. There is a great difference, of course, between the image of an untutored savage and the image of an Einstein. A rough notion of his immediate territory in the case of the first expands into the extended and complex relational image of the second. Even so the gap between the simplest human image and the most complex image of the lower animals is even more enormous; only man, for instance, has a clear image of time, of his own birth and death; only man is able to develop complex relational images and measurements.

Within the image a distinction may be made between the "image of fact" and the "image of value." The image of fact is the "field" of the image — the world of space, time, objects, persons, and relationships. The image of value consists of an *ordering* of parts of the field of the image. By an ordering I mean simply the arrangement of the objects or parts of the field of the image in a rank order — first, second, third, etc., like a class list. There are many images and scales of value — many different orderings, that is, of various parts of the field of the image. Thus the scale may be aesthetic — building A is ranked above building B on the scale of beauty. The scale may be hedonistic: sausage gives me more pleasure than bacon. Without getting into the subtleties of pleasure and pain, the scale may be one of simple personal preference — I prefer the Volkswagen to the station wagon. It may be a scale of ethical value: I may rate one pattern of life ethically superior to another. The scales may have various referents: I may say, for instance, that A is better than B for me, but that B is better than A for my community, or my country, or the world at large. It is clear that there are a large number of value scales, many of which overlap, and which order different parts of the field of the image: the concept of an ordering, however, is common to them all. We do not have to suppose that the whole field of the image is ordered in value scales. Many value scales consist only of "first, second, also ran." Over large parts of the field we are indifferent; all the objects rate equally, which is really to say there is no value scale at all. At different times and places the value scale spreads over different parts of the field. Thus among astrologers I suppose that

Saturn is regarded as a "worse" planet than Venus. I confess I am homocentric enough to think Earth a "better" planet than distant and chilly Pluto, but for the most part I throw no value ordering over the solar system. Most Americans, I imagine, regard the Russian satellites as "worse" than the American variety, and Russians no doubt reverse this order; future generations may class such value orderings with those of astrology. No matter what and when the valuation process, however, and no matter how lofty or how low its frame of reference, the process itself always consists in matching a set of ordinal numbers with parts of the field.

My main interest in *The Image* was the theory of behavior, rather than of the image itself. I suppose there that the behavior of organisms or organizations consists not in a mechanical stimulus-response pattern, but rather in a response to the image. A *decision* involves the selection of part of the field of the image representing the possible future which is highest valued (first in the ordering) of the dominant value ordering. Stated a little less carefully, we might say that an organism moves towards the highest valued part of its image of the future. Thus as long as in my image of space and time my home has the first place in the dominant ordering, I stay at home: when, say on Monday morning, my office has the highest value, I go to the office. Sometimes strange places like New York or South Bend move into top place, on certain dates, and I accordingly move to these places and times. What is true of my behavior, however, is no less true of the lowly amoeba, as it rejects the grain of sand and embraces the grain of food. The concept of the *dominant* value ordering involves the further concept of an ordering of the value orderings themselves. Thus from the point of view of sheer fleshly pleasure I may rate staying in bed on Sunday morning higher than going to church: from the point of view of ethical conduct I rate going to church higher than staying in bed. Which I do depends on which of these value orderings is itself rated highest; the fleshly man stays in bed, the ethical man goes to church. In any case, behavior is quite incomprehensible without a complex of value orderings: a mere image of fact will never lead to behavior, but merely to vegetative inactivity in any place where one falls.

We can now go on to inquire how the image — both of fact and of value — is formed. At this level of analysis I simply avoid the question of the psycho-physical material substance of the image, which is just as well because we know practically nothing about it! That there is some relation between the cognitive content of the image and the material architecture of the nervous system I do not doubt, but what this relation is I do not know, nor does any other mortal know. I am sure that the relation is highly complex, and the evidence suggests that in ways we cannot now visualize the correspondence between the mental content and the molecular and electrical structure of the organism is a correspondence of wholes rather than of parts, in a type of system which as yet we simply do not understand. Be that as it may, the problem of psycho-physical correspondence is fortunately irrelevant at the level of abstraction at which I am operating.

The raw material of the image consists of *information inputs* — information simply being defined as improbable patterns without further inquiring patterns of what substance. Information inputs come from two sources: some come from outside the organism, or rather from outside the image itself, from sense receptors, proprioceptors, or even from more subtle sources. Some however come from within the image itself. This self-generation of messages by the image is the work of the *imagination,* which "bodies forth the forms of things unknown." This self-generation of messages is peculiarly the property of the human image: there may be foreshadowings of it among the higher animals, but it is not until the image and the corresponding messages become largely symbolic in nature that the imagination can develop. This distinction between symbolic and non-symbolic messages is of great importance, and is perhaps the most important single distinguishing mark which separates mankind from the animals. Thus suppose I am in a room and hear a voice speaking behind me. I interpret the sound waves which reach my ear, and the corresponding disturbance, whatever it is, in the nervous system, first of all as a *sign* of someone's presence in the room: I may even recognize the voice as that of an old friend. A dog can do as much. When, however, I listen to what the voice is saying, and understand that the person is talking about things of which I have no direct knowledge, and perhaps no previous knowledge; when the voice describes places where I have never been so that I can picture them, or relates experiences which I have never had, or abstract relations which I have never previously understood, the messages are symbolic. This is an experience denied even to the most intelligent of the lower animals.

One of the interesting things which has emerged from modern studies of perception is that what we usually think of as "sense data" are not "data" at all, but are highly learned interpretations of sense messages which are fitted together into our images of time and space. This learning goes on in early infancy — probably from birth, or even before — so that we are not much conscious of it. The learned character of the interpretation of sense messages is shown by people who, for instance, receive their sight as a result of an operation in adult life after having been blind from birth. It often takes months, or even years, for these people to fit their new sense into their old world; they indeed see "men as trees walking" even though physiologically their sight may be perfect.

Messages, whether from internal or external sources, may affect the image in four ways. Most of the innumerable messages which impinge on us in the course of a day simply pass right "through" the image, like an electron through a molecule, without changing it. Most sense messages, especially when the body is not in motion, make little or no impact on the image of the room where we are sitting. As every teacher knows, a great many symbolic messages likewise are capable of passing through the structure of the student's image and leaving it unscathed! In the second place the message may simply add to the structure of the image, as in rote learning; we learn in school that the sun is 93 million miles from the earth (probably without examining the evidence very closely!) and ever afterwards we can regurgitate this "fact" on call. In a somewhat more involved way messages may extend or clarify our existing images, without producing any fundamental reorganization. Thus we visit a new place: we have an indistinct idea of what it is going to be like before we go, but having been there and seen it we now have a clearer and more distinct image of it. Finally messages may hit some kind of "nucleus" of the image and effect a drastic reorganization. This happens in a dramatic form in conversion: it happens on a smaller scale when we re-evaluate a person, a situation, or a theory. This may be called the "restructuring" of the image.

The image exhibits a good deal of resistance to restructuring, especially where the parts involved are high on some significant value scale. Thus suppose messages reach me to the effect that a highly valued friend, whom I have previously pictured as an upright and honorable man, is in fact a scoundrel. My first impulse is to reject the messages as untrue; my image of the authority of the messages, or of the source of the messages, may be easier to shift than the image of my valued friend. Suppose now however that similar messages come from many different sources, and from sources which I have hitherto always found to be reliable. As these messages cumulate there comes a point where I can no longer accept the "messages are untrue" explanation of the incompatibility between the messages and the image, and my image of my friend undergoes a drastic reorganization. The resistance of the image to restructuring must not be regarded as necessarily undesirable; indeed, were there not such resistance the world would dissolve into a kaleidoscope of meaningless and contradictory messages. Nowhere do we see this more clearly than in sense perception: we only get along in the world by constantly disbelieving the clear evidence of our senses. Thus we do not believe that the stick becomes bent when we put it in water, and if the pattern of an automobile on our retina is growing larger we do not interpret this to mean that the automobile is suffering a strange and uniform increase in size — we get out of its way fast! Similarly we interpret a constantly shifting pattern of lines and shadows as a quite stable and stationary room, even as we walk across it; we interpret another shifting pattern of light and shade and sounds as a person, and so on. In the realm of theories and ideas also we progress towards knowledge only as we hold reasonably fast to that which we have; the person who is blown about by every wind of doctrine, and who is convinced by everything that he hears or reads no matter how contradictory to his previously held opinions, is not likely to proceed to a mature and well-considered point of view.

On the other hand too great resistance to restructuring of the image is also dangerous, and is a sign of mental ill-health. At the extreme we have the schizophrenic whose image is so tight and self-consistent that it resists all change, so that all messages which are inconsistent with it, whether external or internal, are simply rejected out of hand. In extreme cases even sense messages are controlled by the image, so that the unfortunate person only sees, hears or even touches what his image tells him, and he retreats into a world of hopeless hallucination, having lost touch altogether with the "real" world both outside him and within. There are many pre-schizophrenic types in active life, of which the fanatical communist is a good example, whose images are so rigid that no contradictory message can get through to them.

Where the image does change and grow, and is from time to time restructured we must look to the inconsistencies for an explanation — either inconsistencies between various parts of the image, which come to be perceived through the internal message system, or inconsistencies between messages and the image. Just what constitutes inconsistency, however, is hard to spell out. Logical inconsistency is only one aspect; many people seem to have quite stable images which are logically inconsistent! There seems to be a kind of aesthetic consistency which at times dominates "mere" logic, or perhaps constitutes a higher logic. Then there is perhaps some over-all valuation function of the image — that wherever reorganization threatens to give us a "worse" image in some over-all sense it is strongly resisted, and hence the stable image will exhibit something like a maximum of over-all value, at least in the small.

II

I now come to the main thesis of this paper, which is that the value image — that is, the various ordering systems by which the parts of the field of the image are ranked — is created and developed, added to and restructured in much the same way that the "image of fact" or the field of the image is itself created and developed. From the point of view of the genetics and growth of the image, therefore, there is not a sharp distinction between the image of fact and the image of value: both are an integral part of the image, both exhibit consistencies and inconsistencies, both are capable of addition and of restructuring, and the growth patterns of both are always limited by the nature of the messages received and by the nature of the existing image. It is highly probable that in the growth of the organism from its very beginnings in the fertilized egg images both of fact and of value are present together; were this not so it is difficult to see how growth or any form of organic behavior could be possible. The gene clearly carries some kind of a blueprint even in the earliest stages; it certainly has "know-how" of a most elaborate kind, even if it does not have conceptual knowledge, nor does it seem to have any learning ability. Furthermore this "know-how" implies a value image: there are some lines of cell growth which it "prefers" and others which it cuts off in the sculpture of the organic structure. How the gene does this we do not know: from what it does, however, we must presuppose something not wholly unlike, though still very different from a "decision process." Once the organism has developed to the point of awareness, even far below the self-conscious level, it is aware of comfort and discomfort, danger and safety, and these constitute primitive value orderings according to which it moves in its dimly perceived world. Even in such lowly organisms as the molds and slimes we observe behavior which seems inexplicable without some kind of primitive awareness and a primitive value ordering of some complexity, as when large numbers of free cells come together to form complex and differentiated spore-bearing structures.

As we move towards the symbolic and self-conscious level of organization the image correspondingly becomes enormously more complex, in its valuational aspects as well as in its over-all field. At lower levels the value image may be confined to some kind of comfort-discomfort or pleasure-pain scale, though even at these levels it may be more complex than we think — there is self-sacrifice in the interests of a higher cause, for instance, even at the level of the cell! No matter what the biological origins, however, it is clear that as we approach the symbolic and self-conscious image in man the value image also becomes symbolic, and is increasingly divorced from the simpler biological values. On the one hand this leads to people starving in the midst of an abundance of nutritious but unaccustomed food, and on the other hand to the noblest behavior of the martyr or the saint. In man there is a strong tendency for the symbolic image — those things which we have learned by hearing the words or symbols of others — to become dominant. Where there is a complex hierarchy of value orderings, however, the "lower" ones can never be wholly neglected; at the unconscious level or under stress they may take over, and human behavior is nearly always the result of a complex pattern of intersecting and shifting value systems. Purity of heart, alas, is one of the rarest of virtues, and when this purity is obtained by throwing out the higher value systems, it can become pure evil.

We have observed that the growth of the image depends not only on the messages received, but also on its present structure, for present structure always sets some kinds of limits on future growth; thistle seeds do not grow into fig trees, puppies do not grow up into lions, firms rarely grow into churches, or churches into nations, or banks into hospitals. As a special case of this general principle we are coming increasingly to realize that the growth of the image of fact in any individual is governed in part by his existing value orderings, and that change in value orderings likewise is governed in part by reorganizations of the image of fact. This is true, as we noted earlier, even in what we used to think of as "simple" perception. We see the world the way we do, instead of in some possible alternative way, because in some sense it "pays" us to do so. In the theory of signal detection, for instance, it has been shown that the chance of a person detecting a signal, failing to detect it, or giving a false alarm, depends on the "payoffs" (rewards or punishments, or value orderings) associated with each contingency. If penalties for false alarms are great, or rewards for correct interpretations are small, there will be few false alarms but also many "misses." Thus we might almost say that we learn to interpret the barrage of messages from the senses as a three-dimensional world of space and a one-dimensional world of time because if we do not do this we bump into things and hurt ourselves!

Thus in the development of the image a large part is played by a process which might be called *confirmation*. Because the image always includes relations, it can be used as an instrument for predicting the consequences of behavior decisions. Thus if I have an image of a room with myself in it at a certain spot, and also a (largely subconscious) image of my powers of walking, I can decide to walk across the room; my image then includes a prediction of what will happen to the messages I receive as I carry out the decision. If the messages as observed and recorded do not correspond to the images as predicted, then the image is extremely likely to be revised. Suppose, for instance, that as I start to walk across the room, I suddenly run into an invisible wall. It is clear that the messages do not correspond to the prediction, and the image must be revised. I conclude, perhaps, that what I thought was a room was in fact a mirror, or a picture, or perhaps I conclude that there actually is an invisible wall across it. In any case, my previous image is bound to be revised, because of "disappointment" — that is, the failure of predictions to be confirmed. If the prediction is confirmed, then of course the image which gave rise to it is reinforced. A prediction which leads to decision and action, however, always implies that the field of the prediction has a value ordering. If I decide to walk across the room, it is because I want to get to the other side, like the celebrated hen in the riddle. This means that the other side of the room at that time is higher on my value scale than the place where I am. If now my prediction is disappointed, whether by bumping into an invisible wall or by finding that when I get to the other side of the room I don't like it there at all, the value image as well as the field is reorganized. I may decide that the other side of the room is not where I want to be and this side comes uppermost in the value ordering. A good deal of the fabled wisdom of the East consists in the good advice to want what you get rather than to try to get what you want, on the grounds that it is easier to change the value ordering than to encounter repeated disappointments in the field. We see therefore the total image built up as a result of a complex process of message reception, reorganization, prediction, confirmation and disappointment, in which the value image and the image of fact are continuously and inseparably intertwined.

The elaborate images of science are no exception to this rule. The processes of confirmation here are more elaborate, and the value orderings perhaps less explicit than in ordinary life. Scientists form a subculture within the larger society, and this subculture has its own prevalent value orderings. A theory gains acceptance if it rates above competing theories in the value ordering of the

scientific subculture: we can say if we like that those theories succeed which are "pleasing" to the scientist — bearing in mind that
this "pleasing" is not merely an arbitrary emotional glow, but involves the fulfillment of certain rather elaborate predictions, the
development of certain proved attitudes, and the ability to com-
mand a hearing. Even science however is not exempt from sociology, especially on matters where perception is difficult. The extreme dependence of marginal perceptions on the value orderings
of the perceiver raises difficulties even in astronomy, where it has
been suggested that the long controversy over the existence of canals
on Mars may be due to the fact that only the sharp-eyed young can
see them, whereas the dimmer-eyed old have the professorships and
carry the prestige! The difficulties of research into extra-sensory
perception arise out of much the same situation.

III

To say that all images arise from the complex interaction of mes-
sage-inputs with the existing image of fact and of value does not
mean, of course, that there is no distinction between fact and fancy,
illusion and falsehood, right and wrong. It must be emphasized
that the image can be considered at many different levels of abstraction. In the foregoing I have been dealing with it as an object
of observation, and discussing the principles which govern its origins and growth much as one might discuss, say, the principles
which govern the origins and growth of an organization, or of a
plant. I have not said anything — and on the whole I shall try
(probably unsuccessfully) to avoid saying anything about the ultimate truth of the image. Epistemology here faces a very serious
dilemma, that what is *meant* by the "truth" of an image is the correspondence between the image and some reality outside it, which
would continue to exist no matter whether anyone had an image
of it or not: to this extent I am a correspondence theorist. On the
other hand we can never in fact compare an image with an external reality, for all we can ever compare are images with images.
The truth of an image must always be in some sense an inference.
Questions of truth and falsehood therefore can also be discussed

at various levels of abstraction, below the ultimate level of correspondence with external reality.

The image is not arbitrary; it makes a difference whether we hold "truer" or "falser" images, even though absolute truth may elude the purely rational grasp. If my image, for instance, tells me that gravity does not exist, and in consequence I jump off a cliff, then no matter how elevated my thoughts on the way down something fairly unpleasant is likely to happen at the bottom. There are images, that is, which lead to disaster, and others which, we hope, do not. At one level, it certainly seems legitimate to call those which do not lead to disaster "truer" than those which do. In this rather narrow and abstract sense, however, it is clear that value images are just as much subject to judgments of truth and falsehood as are images of fact. If my value ordering is based exclusively on my immediate physical sensations of comfort, so that I always value the immediately comfortable more highly than the immediately uncomfortable, and model my behavior accordingly, this also will lead to disaster, simply because it is sometimes necessary to be uncomfortable in order to survive. Similarly if my value ordering is confined entirely to the states of my own person, so that I treat all others merely as means to my own ends, this too is likely to lead to disaster in the complex interaction of social relations and personal character, for without love the human organization shrinks, decays, and eventually disintegrates.

Let me make quite clear that I am not *equating* survival value, or even the mere absence of disaster, with ultimate truth. I do not presume in this essay to inquire into the ultimates and absolutes. What I am arguing is that on the humbler ground where "truer and falser" in regard to the image relate merely to the pragmatic workability of the image, there are processes of validation even if there is no automatic touchstone of truth, and that *these processes of validation apply just as much to the value image as they do to the image of fact.* At this level, at any rate, the "knowledge of value" is not a different kind of thing from the "knowledge of fact"; both are arrived at by much the same kind of processes, both are an integral and necessary part of the image, both are worked out and tested in behavior, in prediction, in consequences, in confirmations, both grow and develop in the way that the whole image grows and develops. It is a leap of faith, of course, from this proposition to the proposition that the knowledge of values is knowledge of a real, objective world, and that values can be true or false in the sense of correspondence to some outside reality. This leap of faith, however, is no greater than the one required in believing that the image of fact likewise corresponds to a real, objective world and that knowledge of fact likewise implies that there is something there to know. In neither case can we ever compare directly the image with the correspondent reality, for as we have seen only images can be compared with images. In both cases, however, there are processes of validation or confirmation, some of which operate on very simple, unsophisticated, common sense levels and others of which require an elaborate theoretical system and experimental controls.

Even though the processes of validation are much the same in all parts of the image, the difficulties of validation differ markedly from one part to another. There are some parts of the image where validation is easy, as, for instance, in the common-sense image of objects in space and time, because confirmations are direct and rapid. There are other parts where validation is difficult because of the complexity of the relations involved and the slowness with which they operate. Ease of validation usually results in extensive *agreement* about the image — that is, the image is a public image widely shared by indefinitely large numbers of people. Where validation is difficult there is more likely to be disagreement: the public image breaks up into subcultural groups, with each subculture bearing a public image which is shared by its own members but not with others. Here again I do not want to equate the existence of a widespread public image with its ultimate truth: one cannot deny the possibility that widely shared images may be wrong. Forty million Frenchmen *can* be wrong; even an image which is shared by the whole human race *might* be wrong. Nevertheless the wide sharing of a public image is part again of the *process* of validation, even if it is not an infallible test of truth.

A peculiarly difficult problem arises for epistemological theory — and indeed, for social and mental health — in the case of *self-validating images*. Self-validating images are of two kinds. There are those which validate themselves because they control the process of validation in the individual; these might be called self-justifying *illusions*. There are others which validate themselves because they give rise to a corresponding reality outside the image; the image creates the world to which it corresponds. The self-validating image in its first form is perhaps the most distinguishing mark of mental illness. The schizophrenic actually sees, hears, and even touches the illusions which his diseased image bodies forth: the paranoid who thinks that everyone is his enemy interprets even kindness as hidden hostility, and no matter *what* he experiences he will interpret it into his diseased and distorted image. Frequently, however, a diseased image creates its own reality: the paranoid not only misinterprets friendship as hostility; because he does this he behaves in such a way that friendship *turns* into hostility. Indeed, part of the psychological treatment of mental disease consists in creating an "artificial" environment for the patient in which "reality" in the shape of professionalized personal relationships remains unaffected by the patients' behavior, so that the self-validating *social* process at least is cut off. One finds similar phenomena in economic and political life: the "paranoid" nation that believes that everyone is hostile towards it acts in such a way as to transform what may have been initially an illusion into a reality — everybody does become hostile towards it! Similarly in economic life, if everyone believes there is going to be an inflation, individuals seek to protect themselves against this by trying to shift their assets out of money and into goods or stocks, and the result, of course, is the very inflation which was feared. Similarly the fear of depression can lead to one, the fear of war can lead to one, the fear of dictatorship can lead to one. A large part of the problem of social institutions and policy consists in setting up institutional barriers to these self-justifying processes — stabilization devices in economics, federal government in politics, and so on.

The phenomenon of self-justifying images also crops up in the value image. Indeed, it is not too much to claim that every culture is built around a set of value images which the culture then proceeds to protect by setting up institutions of validation. Because of the symbolic nature of much of the value image in man, much of its validation likewise comes from symbolic sources — especially from the approval or reproof of those whose good opinion is important to us. An important part of the confirmation of value images lies in the perception of congruence between the value images of the person and those of the "reference group" with which he is surrounded. In a closed group therefore the value image is likely to be fairly stable, and is perpetuated from generation to generation by the institutions which support and propagate it — the family, the church and the school. The situation is not as simple as this, of course: in the experience of the growing child strong ambivalences are developed, especially under the stricter regimes of child-rearing, and *rebellion* is not infrequent, with rejection of the value image of the culture and the acceptance of competing images: even children reared in a good Catholic environment occasionally become Quakers, and *vice versa!* If, however, the subculture can eject the rebels and if it has a sufficiently high birth and conversion rate, it can maintain itself even in the midst of strong and even hostile competing cultures. The astonishing persistence of the Amish eighteenth-century culture in the midst of the aggressive secular culture of modern America is a case in point. Incidentally, this perhaps explains in part why the church in a monoreligious culture like that of Scandinavia or Spain compares very unfavorably in internal vigor with the same churches in a polyreligious culture like the United States. In a monoreligious culture the church has to absorb its rebels; in a polyreligious culture it can easily eject them.

To say that the value image is partly self-validating within a culture is neither to condemn it nor to deny its ultimate validity. We have seen that even in the image of fact some degree of rigidity is necessary if the image is not to collapse into a jelly of unorganized information. There is unquestionably some optimum point or range of rigidity and degree of self-validation in the value image as well as in the image of fact. The firm structure which is not impervious to challenge seems to be the desirable form. And there is certainly no lack of challenge to the value image, even within fairly tight and closed subcultures. The challenge, especially in a pluralistic society, may come from an outside culture. A good example of a change in the value image of a culture under such challenge is the development of an explicit social ethic in both Catholic and Protestant

Christianity in the latter half of the nineteenth century, a movement which is certainly not unrelated to the challenge of secular social faiths, whether liberal or socialist. The challenge may even come from a *past culture;* the challenge of Greece and Rome as revealed in their surviving literature and architecture had a lot to do with the Renaissance, and the challenge of Biblical Hebraic culture as embodied in the Bible had something, at least, to do with the Reformation. This is perhaps one reason for the paradox that a culture which rests heavily on sacred scriptures and records of the past is often so surprisingly dynamic and vigorous: the constant challenge of the past on the present continually renews it. The challenge may also come from prophetic individuals within the culture. There are from time to time in history individuals who are not caught in the deterministic dynamics of their own culture, but who seem to have access to outside reservoirs of moral reality. We are here approaching the phenomenon of Revelation.

From all these sources, challenges continually come to existing value systems; the challenge, of course, may be rejected, or it may be accepted in whole or in part. It is not difficult to see in this process something strongly akin to the general process of validation of the image, difficult and complex and long drawn out as the process may be. At least in this regard we travel hopefully. It is only proper humility to confess that we know very little about the ultimates and absolutes: it is sheer cowardice, however, to maintain with some modern philosophers that these matters are of no concern to us, or are "nonsense propositions" not worth troubling our minds about. We are not given perfect knowledge, but it is not unreasonable to hope for sufficient knowledge. When this is perceived, it is cause for thankfulness and adoration.

IV

This brings me, very briefly, to the last part of my title. If the subject of the knowledge of value is a touchy one, that of the value of knowledge is doubly so. It is almost treason in the groves of academe to suggest even that the question exists. It is part of the value image of the academic community that any extension of knowledge, in any direction, by anybody, is intrinsically good, and that more knowledge is always to be preferred to less. As far as this is a prejudice, I must confess that I think it is a noble prejudice, and it is one that I share. I detest secretiveness; I harbor the feeling that no decent person would *want* to do classified research whether for government or business, however much other values might impel him towards it. The concept of an open fellowship of seekers after knowledge is one of the most precious gifts of science; by comparison the beastly secretiveness of the totalitarian or military state, or of the mystagogue or the quack is repugnant to the mind and spirit.

Nevertheless there is a problem of the *economy* of knowledge. In the modern world especially we cannot know everything. We are hampered not only if we know things that aren't so, but also if we know things that aren't *necessary*. What is "necessary" is of course a tricky and delicate question, and the above proposition is capable of monstrous perversion. We do *not* want a world of slick technicians, trained rather than educated, knowing only their own little corner of the universe and indifferent to the great concerns and cosmic responsibilities of man. There is a famous passage in Sherlock Holmes where the good Watson reproves the Master for his ignorance of astronomy, and Holmes defends himself by saying that he cannot afford to carry any surplus knowledge in his profession, and that the question of whether the sun goes round the earth or the earth goes round the sun is a matter of utter indifference to him. In that argument I confess I am on the side of Watson! There. are things which we should know simply because of our status as men — these are the things which are the proper core of liberal ˣ education. What these things are, of course, is open to discussion, and the need to replace the mediaeval synthesis with a new trivium and quadrivium appropriate to the vastly expanded knowledge of our day is one of the central questions of modern education. This core of necessary knowledge, however, is a minimum, not a maximum. Even as we go on into the specialized disciplines the problem of the necessary core remains; if we insist on what is not necessary we are doing grave harm to the educational process. What this means is that the growth of the image itself is subject to the evaluative and critical process; the value ordering extends not only over the existing field, but over potential future fields. At some points, much as I hate to admit it, ignorance is, if not bliss, at least good economy. This is a problem which has received too little attention in the academic community, perhaps because each specialist has a strong vested interest in his own specialty and tends to think that this, at least, must be part of the necessary core of knowledge! We must come to recognize, however, that the planning of a curriculum is an ethical problem, and that the more clearly this is recognized, and the more earnestly explicit value systems and ethical principles are sought after in this regard, the more likely we are to achieve "balanced growth" (that elusive ideal of the economics of development!) in knowledge.

Chapter III

Notes on Culture and Ethics

BY CHRISTOPHER DAWSON

1. Ethics have always held an important position in relation to the social sciences. Aristotle treated Ethics as a part of Politics so that ethics and politics formed the two parts of one study. In modern times, with J. S. Mill and his contemporaries, the social sciences were termed "the moral sciences," and modern sociologists and ethnologists like Westermarck have aspired to write "The History of Moral Ideas."

In the United States, above all, the social sciences have tended more and more to study ethics not as an independent discipline, but as a subordinate element, in their attempts to create an all inclusive science of the social process and of human culture.

Thus American sociology from the days of W. G. Sumner has based its approach on the study of the "Folkways" and "Mores," which are regarded as the basic forces in social life and as underlying and creating conscious moral values and standards of behavior.

Similarly American anthropologists by concentrating their attention on the study of *culture* have been led increasingly to study the moral structure of particular cultures and the values or systems of values which distinguish one culture from another. Yet what they are studying is not the ethical but the sociological significance of these values, just as a historian may study the currency systems of different societies without necessarily considering the question of their material wealth or poverty.

2. Meanwhile philosophic ethics (especially in England, per-

haps), have concentrated their attention on the problems of individual morality and the nature of moral obligation. They have become less and less interested in what men do and more and more in why they do it. Now there is no reason why there needs to be a conflict between the philosophers who analyze the nature of the moral act and the anthropologists who study different moral orders and the relation between a culture and its standards of value. In fact, however, there is a serious schism between the philosophers and the social scientists, since the latter tend to emphasize the non-rational customary character of moral standards, while the former regard this procedure as merely explaining away the problems with which their study is concerned.

3. Now there is no doubt that there is a real contradiction between the naive ethical relativism of sociologists like Sumner, who regard moral values as an artificial rationalization of unconscious social habits, and the ethical absolutism of the metaphysicians and the theologians. But I think there is more to be said in favor of the cultural relativism of the anthropologists, since this provides a bridge, or a field for mutual understanding, between the two opposing positions. For in the first place we should note that the moral analysts are themselves prepared to accept the principle of cultural relativity in a limited sense. E.g., J. D. Mabbott in his discussion of the logic of Moral Rules [1] writes: "The duty of a Briton to help the police to arrest a murderer and the duty of a Corsican to kill a member of the murderer's family are basically the same rule of requiting murder, applied to two different sets of circumstances."

4. No doubt the anthropologist regards the concept of culture as amounting to much more than "a set of circumstances." But on the other hand he may be even more dissatisfied with Sumner's conception of the completely non-rational, instinctive character of the folkways, "having the nature of the ways of other animals," and formed by accident, that is to say, by irrational and incongruous action, based on pseudo knowledge.

For even the most primitive culture is entirely "human"; it is due to human continuity — to man's power of symbolic communi-

---

1. In Proc. of the British Academy, 1953, p. 99.

cation by the gift of language. Therefore all the essential components of the culture process — religion and art, ethics and law — are present in culture from the beginning; and no amount of research can ever reveal a pre-moral or pre-religious phase of human development, any more than it can discover a humanity without language. And as language is always acquired, and is not inborn, so too the whole body of culture and cultural institutions, technology and art, education and tradition, law and ethics, religious rites and beliefs, as well as the material apparatus of culture, have been learned and acquired and communicated — not produced, as Sumner seems to suggest, as an instinctive, unconscious reaction to natural forces.

Thus social anthropology in no way underestimates the importance of ethics nor does it try to devaluate or explain away their distinctive character. On the contrary it is through the study of the ethical values and standards of a culture that we can best understand its inner form, the *ethos* or spirit of the culture, to use a common expression.

5. At the same time we cannot deny that anthropology stresses the relative character of ethics, for the values and standards that the anthropologist studies are not abstract values and standards, but the values and standards of particular cultures. Here there is an obvious ground of disagreement between the anthropologist and the ethical philosopher, since the latter is concerned with the internal analysis of the moral behavior of the individual while the former concentrates his attention on an objective inquiry into the values and standards of societies and civilizations.

Yet it should be remembered that the social aspect of ethics has always been important and formerly tended to be predominant. In the past and above all in primitive societies, ethics do not stand alone. They are closely related to three or four other concepts — manners and customs, laws and rites — which are now quite distinct, but which formerly constituted three provinces of one moral kingdom. The change is most obvious in the case of manners, which today are clearly distinguished from ethics, but which were formerly almost indistinguishable. Even the Romans, who were exceptionally interested in moral philosophy and aware of ethical problems, still had one word for the two concepts, so that to the Roman *boni mores* stood primarily for good morals without excluding "good manners." And even today we cannot ignore the close relation and parallelism between moral education and training in good manners, so that children do not distinguish very clearly between the guilt of a moral offense and the shame of a breach of good manners.

Similarly in the case of law, the distinction between the moral and the legal code is relatively late; and not merely in primitive cultures, but in the historic civilizations of the ancient world, the great legal codes were all-inclusive, and they possessed a sacred character which conferred the same ultimate sanction on the prescriptions which we should regard as secular, public or political, as on those which seem to us religious, moral or ceremonial.

This unification of standards is familiar to us historically in the case of the Hebrew *Torah*. Here the unification of religion, ethics, law and rites and ceremonies is peculiarly clear, and it also shows us how this sacred law is regarded as the foundation of the national culture and the very essence of the people's identity.

But there is a similar relation between religion, law, ethics and rites in the great world cultures of China, India and Islam, as well as in more primitive societies.

6. In all these cases ethical values and standards are intimately related to culture. Does this involve a theory of cultural relativism? Here it is necessary to distinguish, since "cultural relativism" is a most equivocal expression and the source of much confusion and misunderstanding. On the one hand, (A) it may mean that man's values and standards are related to his culture, as stated above; on the other hand, (B) it may mean that all cultural values are relative, in the sense that one culture is as good as another and that all moral values are equivalent. And it is obvious that these two positions are widely different and lead to different conclusions.

7. The first view implies that a culture is essentially a moral order. To take a particular case, the Confucian ethics have been the moral basis of Chinese culture for 2,000 years and unless we take account of them we cannot understand Chinese culture. They are linked on the one hand with Chinese religion and ritual, and on the other with the Chinese polity and social organization. And

they are also inseparably connected with Chinese education and the Chinese tradition of learning. Regarded from this point of view, Chinese culture is an indivisible whole — a web of social and moral relations woven without seam from top to bottom.

8. But if a culture is a moral order, there is no need to discuss the cultural relativity of ethics, since no one has ever denied that moral acts depend upon the moral order. No doubt it means that moral laws differ in different ages and cultures, but this also has generally been admitted, since it is clear that the moral law of the Jews is different from that of the Hindus, and that of the Chinese from that of the Greeks. But when we say this we are really admitting no more than when we say that the religions and philosophies of these peoples or civilizations are different.

9. Does this mean that there is no such thing as absolute truth — no true religion, no true philosophy, no universal morality, no common science? That is the final problem for the philosopher and the theologian; and the answer depends on our ultimate convictions. Personally I am a monotheist. I believe that there is a true religion, a universal morality and a common philosophy and science. But this is not today actually realized. When it is actually accepted and fully admitted, then there will also be one universal world culture or civilization.

10. Meanwhile we are living in a world of competitive universal systems diversified by pockets of particularist survivals. And this world of conflicting cultures is also a world of moral disorder. The failure of the modern world to recognize common moral values is inseparably connected with its cultural and religious disunity. A universal moral order is impossible without a universal spiritual community.

No doubt we may attempt to impose a common international order and a universal economic organization on the world, and their achievement would no doubt provide a favorable basis for moral and cultural unity. But it is very doubtful whether we can succeed because the lack of common moral values makes the task appallingly difficult.

11. We may ask whether it would not have been better to have left politics alone and begun at the other end by attempting to

build up a common moral order and a universal spiritual community on which an international order might be built. This after all is what the missionaries and teachers of religion have actually attempted to do, and insofar as it has been successful it has actually achieved wider unities of moral order. This indeed has been the main cause of the extension of the great world civilizations. But when these greater unities come into conflict with one another, their progress has been checked and slowed down with the result that they have been far outpaced in recent times by the rapid technological and economic expansion of Western civilization.

12. The result of this state of things is an inchoate secular cosmopolitanism combined with moral and religious and cultural particularism. This finds expression on the one hand in the modern cult of nationalism which is an idealization of cultural particularism; and on the other in the philosophic or scientific doctrine of relativism, which is the view referred to as *cultural relativism* (B in par. 6 above).

13. This view ridicules the possibility of the knowledge of absolute truths or values in philosophy, ethics and religion. Its attitude towards scientific truth is less clearly defined.

According to this view, every culture possesses its own values and there can be no comparison between them. All cultures and all moral values are equivalent. That is to say, a culture is not a moral order, but only a *set of folkways* and its moral values and standards are simply subjective idealizations of patterns of behavior which have grown out of man's instinctive reactions to his material environment.

14. No doubt this devaluation of moral values is to some extent due to modern ethnology and anthropology, which have concentrated their studies on the most primitive and backward societies accessible. It is natural in these studies to stress differences rather than resemblances and to emphasize those traits in primitive culture which appear most immoral or irrational to the Western observer: the ways of peoples who eat their grandmothers and sacrifice their children and indulge in rites of sexual promiscuity. And similarly they tended to emphasize the magical as against the moral or spiritual elements in primitive religion.

15. But as knowledge increased, this simplified view of primitive culture gave place to a more balanced appreciation. A deeper and more sympathetic study of primitive culture showed the existence of basic similarities or analogies between the lower and higher cultures. We see that even primitive cultures possess a real sense of *a sacred community* which includes the living and the dead and gives spiritual unity to the tribe or the society. Similarly they possess a sense of *sacred order* which is both moral and ritual and imposes strict sanctions on both social and individual behavior. Finally they all believe in *the existence of transcendent divine or supernatural powers* and in the importance of maintaining right relations with them as an indispensable condition of human welfare.

16. Now all these three concepts also form an integral part of the higher religions and the world cultures with which those religions are associated. No doubt they are not characteristic of the modern secularized version of Western culture which has become world-wide, but insofar as this is so, it is a source of weakness and not of strength. In fact the lack of these three universal norms gives our modern civilization an incomplete and anarchic character, so that it is a chaos of conflicting ideologies, institutions and standards. The modern world wears the same clothes and drives the same cars, but it does not possess common ethical values or a sense of spiritual community or of religious truth. And thus in our modern world ethical relativity does not mean the necessary relatedness of a culture to its moral order, but the absence of moral order, and the anarchy of competing ideologies and ethical systems.

17. All these conflicts and divisions are potentially capable of resolution, but only on the highest plane. The Divine Word is not only the principle of cosmic order and the source of moral order. He is also the cornerstone of a new and universal social order. This order is a true society and more than a society. It is a new humanity in which all the partial and incomplete forms of human culture find their realization and fulfillment. As St. Augustine writes, "The Church recruits her citizens from all nations, and in every language assembles her community of pilgrims upon earth. She is not concerned about divisions in customs, laws and institutions. She does not exclude or destroy any of them but rather preserves and ob-

serves them. Even the differences of different nations, so long as they do not impede the worship of the one supreme and True God, she directs to the one common end of peace upon earth." [2]

Here then there is a real reconciliation between the principle of cultural relativity and the universality of divine truth and moral order. But it is to be found nowhere else. For "Christ is our peace who has made both one, breaking down the wall of partition" that divided men from one another.

2. *De Civ. Dei,* XIX, cap. 17.

Chapter IV

The Philosophical Presuppositions of
Cultural Relativism and Cultural Absolutism*

BY DAVID BIDNEY

I

The primary concern of the cultural anthropologist is to study the facts of human culture from a naturalistic and humanistic point of view. By definition, culture refers to the historically acquired forms of behavior and thought characteristic of man individually and collectively as a member of society together with the products of this activity designated as artifacts, socifacts and mentifacts. Since different societies have acquired diverse forms of culture, anthropologists refer to each system or configuration of forms as constituting a culture. Thus, by culture in general I shall refer to the art of living evolved by man in society. By a culture I shall refer to the specific modes of actual behavior and thought, to the institutions and social values together with the material, social and mental products of these activities which are shared in whole or in part by members of a given society.

It should be noted, however, that some leading contemporary American anthropologists, notably A. L. Kroeber and Clyde Kluckhohn, differentiate sharply between the actual behavior of man and the abstract forms or patterns of behavior, reserving the term culture for the abstract forms alone. According to these authors, "Whether behavior is to be included in culture remains a matter of dispute. . . . The two present authors incline strongly to exclude

* The writer is indebted to the Wenner-Gren Foundation for Anthropological Research for a grant-in-aid in support of this research.

behavior as such from culture. . . . Culture being basically a form or pattern or design or way, it is an abstraction from concrete behavior, but is not itself behavior. Behavior is, of course, a precondition of culture; just as the locus or residence of culture can only be in the human individuals from whose behavior it is inferred or formulated. It seems to us that the inclusion of behavior in culture is due to confusion between what is a pre-condition of culture and what constitutes culture." [1] Culture is regarded by these authors as a "logical construct" based on actual behavior and behavioral products but "culture is not behavior nor the investigation of behavior in all its concrete completeness." [2] Thus culture has now been reduced from the status of being the highest level of natural phenomena to a logical abstraction, to a thing of reason in the mind of the anthropologist.

As indicated in my *Theoretical Anthropology*, my own position still is that while culture patterns may be considered in abstraction from actual behavior for the purpose of comparative analysis, this does not imply that culture is *nothing but* a logical abstraction of forms and patterns. According to the existential, polaristic theory of culture which I have advocated, culture is constituted by the patterned behavior of man in society; pattern and process are distinguishable but actually inseparable aspects or attributes of cultural behavior. I find it difficult indeed to understand how these same anthropologists continue to speak of cultural processes while maintaining that culture is a logical abstraction; abstractions are not processes. I should be inclined to distinguish between a culture considered as a logical construct in the mind of the anthropologist and the actual, existential culture to which his logical construct refers, just as the physicist distinguishes between the abstract idea of the atom and the actual atom which he can explode into atomic energy. In my opinion, it is Kroeber and Kluckhohn who have confused the concept of culture which is indeed a logical construct, and the actual, existential culture which is a distinctive mode of actual, historic living in human society. Actual, existen-

1. Kroeber and Kluckhohn, *Culture: A Critical Review of Concepts and Definitions,* p. 155. (Complete references are furnished by Dr. Bidney at the end of this chapter—Ed.)
2. *Ibid.,* p. 189.

tial culture is a pre-condition of the abstraction or logical construct in the mind of the anthropologist but there is more to culture than the abstractions of the anthropologist.

Morality is a cultural universal in the sense that all historically known societies have some system of norms and rules for the regulation of interindividual conduct. That mode of conduct which the society approves is called good; that which it prohibits is called evil. Moral norms and institutions are necessary functionally for the survival or self-preservation of any society as well as for the promotion of the well-being or happiness of its members.

For the anthropologist, then, all morality is humanistic and naturalistic because it represents a set of norms and institutions introduced by man for the preservation of his collective existence and the promotion of his virtue and happiness. Morality is an integral part of human culture and is a function or product of human creativity subserving human needs and ends. Morality is relative to man in the sense that human virtue and vice depend upon human powers and potentialities. From a biological point of view this means that human ethics is valid only for man and relative to his specific, differentiating function which, according to Aristotle, consists in the exercise of his potentiality for rational, conceptual thought. Only man among animals is capable of ethical thought and moral behavior because only man is capable of rational deliberation and choice. Even from a theological point of view, the net result of Adam's partaking of the fruit of the tree of knowledge of good and evil was to render him unique in the animal kingdom as the only animal endowed with the potentiality for knowing good and evil and capable of practicing virtue and vice.

Man being by nature a social animal, that is, one who tends to live in societies and communities rather than in isolation from other human beings, morality has been instituted to regulate the life of man in society. This does not mean, however, that ethics is to be regarded solely as a biological means and not as an end in itself. If we assume, as the anthropologist and biologist do, that life is an end in itself, then human virtue is also an end in itself and is its own reward. The end of life is the enjoyment of the life of virtue since the life of virtue involves the exercise of man's distinctive and highest potentialities.

The biological relativity of human ethics implies a concern and even a reverence for human life but not, as Albert Schweitzer has maintained, a reverence for all forms of life in general. We are to treat humanity, according to Kant's categorical imperative, always as an end and never as a means only, but the rest of the animal kingdom may be treated as means to our human ends. This does not indicate that we are to be cruel to animals at will and kill them wantonly for sport; it implies only that we do not extend to animals the same moral recognition that we do to human beings.

The biological relativity of ethics is compatible with the doctrine that human ethics is valid for all mankind as a species and that an ideal or normative ethics is potentially valid for all human societies. In other words, biological relativity implies a *relative absolute,* an imperative valid for only one species of animal, and not one valid for all rational or intelligent beings. As against the Kantian type of ethics which tends to separate the *ought* of moral obligation from any pragmatic considerations, the doctrine of biological relativity of ethics stresses that moral values are evaluated by their consequences for human well-being and that what man *ought to do* is determined by what man as an organism *can do* to realize his highest potentialities.

The question may be raised, of course, whether there is a common or universal human nature and hence whether one may postulate a rational ethics potentially valid for all mankind. The racists who subdivide mankind into "chosen" peoples act as if the attribute of humanity pertains only to their kind of people or "race" and that other peoples may be treated as though they were subhuman. Such a creed leads logically to the practice of genocide, to the extermination of other peoples who interfere with the quest for imperial power and conquest. The theological doctrine of the divine creation of man "in the image of God" and scientific anthropological thought are in complete accord in the assumption of a universal human nature with equal potentiality for participation in the cultural process. The modern institution of a United Nations organization is a practical as well as symbolic recognition of the unity of mankind as a species and the desirability of a common ideal of world civilization.

II

Nineteenth-century anthropologists and sociologists, such as Frazer and Comte, adhered to an evolutionary theory of culture and the ideal of progress. They differentiated, however, rather sharply between religious beliefs and moral values. In accordance with their positivistic thesis, they assumed that religion was essentially a delusion, though a delusion having pragmatic value in enabling prescientific man to face and adjust to the crises of life. Ethics, on the other hand, was held to be objectively valid and to provide a criterion for evaluating human progress and degeneration in culture. The positive science of man called for a science of moral laws and for the moral evaluation of culture history.

With the advent of the twentieth century, the thesis of the cultural evolutionists that there were unilinear, fixed stages of cultural evolution making for cultural progress was subjected to devastating criticism, especially by British and American ethnologists such as Rivers and Boas. Boas, in particular, reacted rather sharply to the tendency of the evolutionists to set up scales of cultural progress applicable to all mankind. In contrast to the monistic theory of cultural evolution involving mankind as a whole, Boas and his followers preferred a pluralistic theory of the history of cultures. The notion that our Western European civilization represents the highest point of cultural development seemed to him obviously ethnocentric and presumptuous. He admitted progress in technological achievement as well as refinement and clarification in conceptual thought but he denied any progress in the sphere of the arts, religion and morality. In contrast to the certainty of the eighteenth-century rationalists and nineteenth-century evolutionists that there was a rational, knowable norm of cultural progress, Boas and his followers denied that there was any such rational and empirical criterion. According to *The Mind of Primitive Man* "The evaluation of intellectual coordination of experience, of ethical concepts, artistic forms, religious feeling is so subjective in character that an increment of cultural values cannot readily be defined." [3]

3. Boas, *The Mind of Primitive Man,* p. 205.

Ruth Benedict's *Patterns of Culture* gave articulate and popular expression to the currently accepted mode of ethnological thought. Historic cultures, whether literate or preliterate, were regarded as aesthetic patterns or configurations, each of which was a legitimate expression of the potentialities of human nature. For Benedict as for Boas, a frank recognition of ultimate cultural disparity and mutual tolerance for the coexisting patterns of culture provide the only scientific and practical basis for intercultural harmony. Each culture was thought to be an integrated whole revealing characteristic patterns, such as the Apollonian and Dionysian patterns which Benedict discerned in some native cultures, but the world of culture as a whole lacked unity; it was a many rather than a one.

This aesthetic and liberal attitude toward the variety of culture systems led to the formulation of a theory of cultural and moral relativisim. In order to explain clearly the philosophical presuppositions of cultural relativism it is necessary to distinguish clearly, as Herskovits has done in part, between (1) the fact of cultural diversity and the fact of ethnocentrism on the part of their respective adherents; (2) methodological relativism in the study of cultures; (3) the philosophic anthropology constructed to explain the facts of the diversity and ethnocentricity of cultures; (4) the pragmatic implications and prescriptions based on the acceptance of a theory of cultural relativism.

We are indebted to modern ethnological research for a greater awareness and appreciation of the fact of the diversity of human cultures. It is now known that adherents of different cultures interpret the data of experience differently and that their perception of phenomena in space and time varies with their cultural conditioning. Furthermore, ethnocentrism, understood as "an attitude of mind characteristic of those who regard their own cultural values as the only valid ones," is a historical fact which may be easily verified by a comparative study of cultures. The Greeks of the time of Herodotus were well aware that "custom is king" and the Hebrews and Persians as described in the Old Testament book of Esther were conscious of the diversity of cultures in the one hundred and twenty-seven kingdoms of Ahasuerus. Modern ethnology, through its comparative, empirical studies of cultural phenomena, has documented these perceptual and ideological differences with much greater detail and precision than ever before.

The methodological implications of cultural pluralism were first developed in modern scientific ethnology. In their quest for a valid, objective method of research, ethnologists have insisted that cultural phenomena are to be understood from the perspective of the adherents of a given culture rather than from the perspective of the observer. This means that cultural phenomena are to be evaluated in terms of their significance in a given cultural and social context. The ethnologist is aware that similar forms of behavior, ritual and belief may have different functional significance in different cultural contexts. The methodology of cultural relativism rests on the assumption that the ethnologist as observer is able to transcend or discount for the moment his own cultural conditioning and to assume the ethnocentric attitude and mentality of one of the adherents or participants in the given culture. This requires a measure of imagination and empathy on the part of the observer in order that he may see others as they see themselves or as they wish to be seen. The observer must be a kind of artist capable of empathy with his subjects and capable of reconstructing their personal experiences in his own mind. The anthropologist Malinowski, in particular, exemplified this kind of sympathetic observation and understanding in his study of the *Argonauts of the Western Pacific* and *Coral Gardens and Their Magic*.

The philosophical anthropology constructed to provide a theoretical foundation for the facts of cultural relativism has varied with the philosophical orientation of the different authors. Thus Nietzsche in his *Genealogy of Morals* transvaluated traditional moral values by indicating how they served the interests of masters and slaves respectively in their quest for domination and foreshadowed the twentieth-century political experiments in Germany and Italy which aimed at substituting the morality of a master-race of "supermen" in place of the "slave" morality of the democratic nations. Similarly the contemporary Communist cultural revolution presupposes the relativity of cultural values to class interests and would replace "capitalistic" and idealistic ethics with "proletarian," materialistic values. The fundamental philosophical assumption underlying sociological determinism and relativism is that society is a newly emergent, self-explanatory reality *sui generis* from which all the modes of social and cultural life are to be derived and through which they are to be explained historically and logically. As may be seen from the work of Durkheim and Sumner, society is viewed as a closed, self-intelligible system which is the source and ground of all sociocultural phenomena. All cultural values are thought to be functions of social organization and to vary with the modes and interests of society.

The fact of cultural relativism has also been explained from an ethnological point of view in terms of a theory of cultural determinism. According to the older theory of the cultural "superorganic" associated with the names of Rivers, Lowie, Malinowski (in part) and Kroeber (in the past), culture as a reality *sui generis* constitutes the highest level of phenomenal reality. This theory presupposes cultural monism since the unity of culture is the culture of humanity as a whole and all particular cultures are regarded as abstractions from this concrete, universal whole. Cultural differences are said to be due to the contingencies of culture history, whereas cultural evolution represents the stages of human development manifested in human culture as a whole. All cultural phenomena are to be explained by other cultural phenomena since culture constitutes a closed system and is self-intelligible. According to the newer theory of cultural pluralism developed independently by Boas and Malinowski, the unit of culture is the particular culture and culture as a whole is an abstraction from the concrete pluralism of actual cultures. Cultural monists and cultural pluralists tended to agree, however, in their theory of cultural determinism which proclaimed culture as the entity and process primarily responsible for the variety of human thought and behavior.

It is worthy of notice in this connection that Melville Herskovits, the most articulate exponent of a theory of cultural relativism, has found support for his approach in the Neo-Kantian, historical idealism of Ernst Cassirer. According to Cassirer's spiritual anthropology,[4] man lives in a symbolic universe of his own creation. There is, for Cassirer, no reality other than the symbolic forms and hence for him all reality is cultural or symbolic reality. Herskovits agrees

---

4. See Bidney, "The Philosophical Anthropology of Ernst Cassirer" in *The Philosophy of Ernst Cassirer*, edited by Schilpp, pp. 465-544.

with Cassirer's conclusion and in his *Cultural Anthropology*[5] writes: "Even the facts of the physical world are discerned through the enculturative screen so that the perception of time, distance, weight, size and other 'realities' is mediated by the conventions of any given group." All reality as known is cultural reality and all human experience is culturally mediated. Hence all cultural evaluations are said to be relative to the cultural background out of which they arise. Herskovits does admit that culture is open to change by individuals but he does not grant that there is any known reality other than cultural reality. When faced with the postulate of an objective reality independent of the observer, he plaintively asks, "Whose objective reality?"[6] thereby committing himself once more to a closed system of cultural determinism.

Herskovits has seen clearly that the theory of cultural relativism is fundamental and that the philosophy of moral relativism is dependent on it. Once it is granted that all reality as known is culturally mediated or conditioned, then it follows that all cultural judgments, perceptions and evaluations are a function of, and relative to, a given cultural system. Moral values, like aesthetic values, are but one element in cultural experience and moral relativism is but one aspect of a general theory of cultural relativism. It is possible, however, to hold to a theory of moral or ethical relativism on psychological grounds without accepting a general theory of cultural relativism. For example, Westermarck maintains in his *Ethical Relativity* that moral evaluations are expressions of individual emotions and have no basis in objective fact. His argument, like that of David Hume, rests on the assumption of the *subjective* origin of value judgments, whereas the cultural relativist maintains that because of the *objective* determinism of culture moral values are relative to the society and culture in which they originate.

The theory of moral relativism rests on two distinct assumptions: First, that all moral evaluations are culturally conditioned or determined and hence that the cultural origin of moral values limits their validity to the social and cultural context in which they origi-

5. *Cultural Anthropology*, p. 35.
6. Herskovits, "Some Further Comments on Cultural Relativism" in *American Anthropologist*, vol. 60, April 1958, p. 271.

nated. Second, it is claimed that it is impossible in practice to establish any universally acceptable criterion for measuring and comparing moral values. Hence each moral system is to be regarded as having equal validity.

This practical assumption of the equality of disparate moral systems leads to the prescription of tolerance as the primary social virtue. *Reverence for culture* rather than reverence for life becomes the absolute, cross-cultural virtue advocated by the cultural relativist. The recognition of the relative validity of one's own values and the assumption of the equal validity of other systems is said to constitute a solid, theoretical basis for mutual tolerance. Intolerance arises from the ethnocentric, uncritical assumption of the absolute and universal validity of one's own cultural values and the denial of such claims in the case of other systems.

It should be especially noted that the cultural and moral relativist does not advocate moral skepticism and nihilism. That, he would say, is a philosophical disease to which he is not subject. Morality is a cultural universal and is essential for the corporate existence of any society. The members of any given society are obligated to conform to the rules and norms of that society on the practical, utilitarian ground that without such obedience social life would be impossible. Each society plays the game of life, so to speak, by different rules but each must have moral rules in order to have any game at all. Pragmatically, the individual must conform to the rules of his society and each society must tolerate the codes of other societies in the interest of mutual survival. Obedience is a cultural imperative once a given code has been accepted.

The practical and political import of cultural and moral relativism appears most clearly in the "Statement on Human Rights" [7] which Herskovits drafted on behalf of the executive board of the American Anthropological Association in 1947 and submitted to the United Nations Commission on Human Rights. In this statement the author submits three basic propositions: (1) The individual realizes his personality through his culture, hence respect for individual differences entails respect for cultural differences; (2) Respect for cultural differences is justified by the fact that no

7. *American Anthropologist*, vol. XLIX (1947), pp. 539-43.

technique of qualitatively evaluating cultures has been discovered; (3) Standards and values are relative to the culture from which they derive so that any attempt to formulate postulates that grow out of the beliefs and norms of one culture must to that extent be invalid for another culture. Any attempt at comparative evaluation presupposes an ethnocentric perspective. That is why the author of and the supporters of this Statement on Human Rights advised the United Nations Commission not to formulate any doctrine of universal human rights; to do so would be to assume the principle of absolute universal human values which they deny on principle.

The only absolute right which the cultural relativist recognizes is the *negative* right to be different and to adhere to one's cultural values. There can be no positive universal rights since "what is held to be a human right in one society may be regarded as antisocial by another people." Hence, it is argued, one must not interfere or intervene in the affairs of another's society since to do so would be to betray one's ethnocentrism and prejudice.

In practice, extreme cultural liberalism and cultural conservativism tend to converge upon a common policy. Cultural relativists who regard themselves as liberals and democrats are opposed to a declaration of universal human rights for fear of interfering with the absolute right to freedom of cultural expression. Extreme conservatives and nondemocrats are opposed to a declaration of human rights because they fear the effect of equalizing social standards upon the established order with its vested interests. Both parties prefer the *status quo* in culture, the one in the name of cultural relativism and democracy, the other in the name of a static cultural absolutism and a fixed, hierarchical order.

III

So far my main concern has been to present the theses of cultural and moral relativism and to explain some of the basic presuppositions which are involved. We turn now to a critical analysis of each of the main arguments previously presented.

First, as regards the facts of cultural relativism and ethnocentrism, I have already indicated that we can have no quarrel with the basic facts of cultural diversity and the evidence reported by ethnologists concerning the role of cultural symbols and institutions in determining perceptual meanings and values. What is questionable, however, is the *extent* of these cultural differences. Evolutionary ethnologists of the nineteenth century stressed the uniformities of culture at given stages of development but failed to appreciate sufficiently the extent of actual, functional differences. By contrast, modern cultural relativists and functionalists stress cultural differences and the functional integration of particular cultures but tend to neglect or ignore the uniformities or common elements. Obviously, if comparative analysis is to be possible at all, we must have some common elements as well as differences. According to Linton, "As the social scientist's acquaintance with a large number of cultures improves, he cannot fail to be more impressed with their similarities than with their differences." [8] The question remains, however, as to the nature of these common elements or similarities.

Herskovits differentiates between cultural universals and cultural absolutes. Universals are "those least common denominators to be extracted from the range of variation that all phenomena of the natural or cultural world manifest." [9] Examples of cultural universals are the family, morality, the enjoyment of beauty and some standard of truth. The cultural categories as empty forms are universal; the actual empirical content varies with each culture. Each culture has its own fixed standards or norms but there are no absolute, universal norms valid for all cultures.

As against this universal formalism of the cultural relativist it may be argued that the actual values reflected in cultural systems are much the same everywhere and that differences arise, as Linton has pointed out, over the relative importance of particular values and the extent of their application. Thus, for all cultures, the perpetuation of the society takes precedence over the life of the individual and hence no society tolerates treason, murder, rape, or incest. All societies recognize mutual rights and duties in marriage and condemn acts which threaten family solidarity. Similarly all

8. Ralph Linton, "Universal Ethical Principles: An Anthropological View," in *Moral Principles of Action,* ed. R. N. Anshen, p. 647.
9. *Cultural Anthropology,* p. 364.

societies give recognition to personal property and provide some techniques for the distribution of economic surplus to the needy. The fact of common cultural values provides a basis for mutual understanding between diverse societies.

The point at issue is whether, following the cultural relativist, we recognize only empty, formal, universal categories of value with unlimited diversity of content, or whether we also grant actual universal values revealed by a comparative study of cultures. As Malinowski and Linton have stressed, there is an actual, common core of cultural values in all societies which derives from the universal functions these values fulfill in satisfying human needs, desires and interests. There are concrete, cultural universals because there are universal needs, biological, derived and integrative, common to all societies. These cultural universals, comprising institutions and values, are not merely abstract categories but actual, regulative modes of conduct and norms of conduct common to all cultures. Such transcultural values implicit in all cultures may be called absolutes as well as universals since they do not vary from culture to culture.

The thesis I would maintain is that not all absolutes are necessarily ethnocentric and that there are transcultural absolutes or cultural imperatives which arise because all human societies share a common, rational, human nature with a variety of needs dictated by their common functions and potentialities. It is important, therefore, to define carefully the meaning of ethnocentrism in order to differentiate clearly ethnocentric absolutes from non-ethnocentric absolutes. Herskovits' definition states that "Ethnocentrism is the point of view that one's own way of life is to be preferred to all others." [10] This definition is not satisfactory since it supposes a priori that *any* preference for one's own culture is necessarily ethnocentric.

I should define ethnocentrism as an attitude of mind and mode of conduct characterized by the adherence to *false* absolute values. The primitive distinction between in-group *versus* out-group is a case in point. To apply moral norms to the members of one's own in-group and to exclude the stranger from moral recognition and

10. *Cultural Anthropology*, p. 356.

treatment as if he were non-human is an instance of arbitrary standards and ethnocentrism. Similarly, to set up any artifact or material means as if it were an end in itself, to value economic goods, for example, as an absolute good irrespective of human costs is to posit a false absolute and any individual or society which adheres to such a false absolute is ethnocentric. To set up any relative good as if it were an absolute good or end-in-itself is to introduce a false absolute. This is the point Spinoza was concerned with in his *Tractatus Theologico-Politicus* when he stated that "nothing is in itself absolutely sacred, or profane, and unclean, apart from the mind, but only relatively thereto." "A thing is called sacred and Divine when it is designed for promoting piety, and continues sacred so long as it is religiously used; if the users cease to be pious, the thing ceases to be sacred; if it be turned to base uses, that which was formerly sacred becomes unclean and profane." [11] Piety is an absolute value or virtue but all acts and artifacts, such as texts, are relative goods whose value is measured by their function in promoting piety. Obviously, ethnocentrism as here defined is a universal, empirical fact and no society is entirely immune from it.

Ethnocentrism manifests itself especially in the form of prejudice against alien cultures and *uncritical* preference for one's own *mores* and culture. For Europeans to judge American culture by its worst traits and to arrogate to themselves alone a true appreciation of spiritual values is ethnocentrism. Americanization, we are informed by reliable reporters, has become a derogatory term in contemporary British, French and German society and what "American" means to Americans is seldom conveyed to the people of these countries. This type of ethnocentric prejudice builds up resistance and anti-American sentiment at the very same time that acculturation in the form of adoption of American inventions, popular music and goods is accelerated. It is not, however, the mere fact of preference for one's own culture that constitutes ethnocentrism but rather the uncritical attitude towards one's own culture and the distorted, biased criticism of alien cultures.

But civilized societies do also have norms which are true absolute values in the sense that they have universal, rational validity while being accepted and preferred by a particular society. For

11. *Tractatus Theologico-Politicus,* ch. XII, p. 167.

example, the moral laws of the Mosaic code with their prohibition of murder, adultery and false oaths, originated in ancient Hebrew society and won acceptance in Western Christian society but this historic fact does not render these norms ethnocentric since they are rational norms with transcultural validity. The Golden Rule is a moral principle which in one form or another has been proclaimed in all civilized societies and transcends the limitations of any one historic culture.

It is necessary to differentiate clearly the ethnocentrism of practice from the ethnocentrism of theory. A society may have a rational moral code but apply it only to its own citizens. Native peoples tend to be ethnocentric in practice since they are largely kinship groups in small societies. On the other hand, the moral norms and beliefs themselves may be ethnocentric in the sense of being subjective, irrational preferences incapable of universal validation and acceptance. Racism or extreme nationalism as a criterion of value is a vicious form of ethnocentrism. Modern totalitarian states suffer from ethnocentrism in theory and practice because they set up false absolutes to the neglect of freedom of thought and freedom of cultural life. The antidote to ethnocentrism with its false absolutes is the conception of true absolutes, that is, rational norms with a potentiality for universal acceptance in the course of cultural evolution. The concept of a single world society and civilization presupposes the concept of absolute norms and rights valid for all mankind. Unless mankind possesses a common core of values and has the ability to transcend the limitations of its historic, ethnocentric values such a program could neither be conceived nor realized.

So long as the attitude of cultural and moral relativism prevails ethnocentrism is unavoidable in principle. If we are told and believe that, in spite of so-called cultural universals, we share no common human perspectives and no common rational values, and that each individual is to adhere to the culture norms of his society because it makes for individual adjustment and social integration, then there is no alternative to ethnocentrism. The members of each society are bound to act as they have been conditioned by their culture and to prefer its values to all others. To say that one *ought not to be* ethnocentric under the supposed conditions of cultural relativism is to ask the impossible. To maintain the relative validity of one's own values requires a comparative, cross-cultural point of view which the individual immersed in his own culture cannot possibly attain. Thus we arrive at the paradoxical conclusion that cultural relativism is the philosophy of those who have themselves transcended actual cultural relativism.

IV

The fundamental epistemological and ontological presupposition of cultural relativism is, as suggested earlier, the notion that reality as known is always cultural reality and that man lives in a cultural, symbolic universe of his own creation. All experience is culturally mediated. There is no reality known to man beyond, or in addition to, cultural reality. All reality as known is culturally determined. Once this basic assumption is granted then it follows *a priori* that all modes of perception and all value judgments are also culturally conditioned since culture constitutes a closed, self-intelligible system. This thesis implies that culture is an *absolute reality* in the sense that culture alone is autonomous and independent, and that all modes of human experience and thought are *relative* thereto because they are functions of culture and dependent on it for their form and content. In sum, *cultural relativism presupposes a theory of cultural absolutism.*

As against the uncritical assumption of cultural relativism that culture is the primary determinant of human experience and that all reality as known is cultural reality, I should maintain that culture is *but one* of the conditions of human experience. As suggested in my *Theoretical Anthropology*, I postulate a *meta-cultural reality* which exists independent of human experience and which is gradually discovered but never fully comprehended in the course of human experience. There is more to this infinite reality than our present, finite cultural categories and concepts make known to us. Like the *Ding-an-Sich* of Kant and the *Substance* of Spinoza, the attributes by which we know reality never exhaust the nature of reality. The phenomenal world is reality as it appears to human scientific perception, or as it may be conceived by the intellect, but the attributes by which we know nature are not the only appearances of reality which exist or which may become known to us as a result of scientific experiment in the future. The modern discovery of the secrets of atomic energy is an instance of such creative discovery.

This postulate of a meta-cultural reality renders scientific progress intelligible and saves us from the *culture-centric predicament* of both historic idealism and historic materialism of never being able to escape from the net of culture. According to the polaristic theory of culture which I have advocated, *nature is absolute and our cultural constructs are the relative means* (which man has invented) by which to "conquer" reality and adjust to it in order to survive. The cultural mentifacts of man may condition him to experience nature in a given traditional way but it is always possible to *decondition* him and for given societies to break through the chrysalis of culture into the realm of nature in order to discover new potentialities in nature and man, undreamed of by their ancestors. These new discoveries will then be expressed in cultural symbols and provide occasion for new institutions until the cycle is repeated once more. In the experimental method of science modern man has discovered the most potent instrument for progressively enlarging his cultural horizons.

Modern social and cultural anthropology have made us aware of the role of social institutions and cultural conditioning in molding the "basic personality structure" of their subjects. The fact of cultural conditioning and the resultant cultural relativism in human experience and perspective must now be regarded as established. The criticism offered here concerns only the *degree* of this cultural determinism and cultural relativism. Culture, I have maintained, is not the only or primary factor in human experience; it is but one essential condition of human experience. The other pole or dimension of reality is that of nature, cosmic and human, which provides human experience with a common frame of reference and enables man to correlate his cultural constructs with the coercive power of nature and his own individual and social needs and desires. The fallacy of cultural relativism consists in regarding culture as if it were an autonomous, absolute, closed system which determines the relative modes of human experience. As against this thesis I have maintained that nature is the absolute reality and the measure of culture, and that culture is the distinctive and relative human means of adjusting to nature and utilizing her powers in the service of mankind.

If culture is understood as a means of adjusting to nature and satisfying human needs and desires, then it follows that no cultural order or system is absolute in the sense of being fixed and valid for all time. The humanistic and naturalistic approach to social institutions which has been characteristic of European culture since the time of the Renaissance has led to a critical, and often revolutionary, appraisal of the established social order. Modern evolutionary anthropology has made us conscious of the historical development of cultures and the functional, instrumental significance of cultures in promoting social solidarity and survival. Utopias as visions of an ideal order have served to draw attention to the limitations of the contemporary social order and to suggest possible alternatives for improvement.

The irony of modern cultural relativism derives from the fact that modern ethnology started out, as we see from Tylor's *Primitive Culture,* as a reformer's science designed to abolish sacred superstitions and myths and to promote cultural progress; but has now reversed itself and has become the advocate of cultural conservatism and reverence for established institutions. The liberalism and humanism with which evolutionary anthropology began has turned to reaction and romantic sentimentalism in the hands of those who have reduced the ideal of progress to narrow ethnocentrism.

Ultimately, the issue involved is a philosophical or meta-cultural one. If the only reality is cultural reality which is relative to the historical experience of different societies, as the cultural and sociological relativists maintain, then indeed the concept of an ideal truth other than the given cultural experience becomes meaningless. As against this position, I maintain that the postulate of objective reality, independent of the observer, is pragmatically a fruitful one, since it serves as a guide to research and to the discovery of new potentialities of nature. Reality as an ontological existent independent of man is an absolute object to which our ideas progressively conform in the course of our quest for knowledge by scientific methods. In the sphere of the social studies, ideal truth represents a norm or goal of human endeavor, a possibility compatible

with human potentialities but one not found in any actual, historical cultural situation. The ideal truths of science and philosophy
are products of cultural experience; yet they transcend the empirical limits of actual cultural experience, and point to a meta-cultural
reality which surpasses anything given in the context of experience.
This leads to the concept of a normative science of culture concerned with the formulation of cultural ideals as possible means
and ends of sociocultural life. The function of a normative science
of culture is to investigate experimentally and suggest new modes
of human conduct which may serve as norms for new cultural institutions and modes of living.[12]

In historical experience, the price of identifying the ideal with
the actual state of culture is intolerance, born of a false absolute.
Once it is asserted that a given cultural system embodies all the
ideal values, then the way is prepared for a justification of intolerance towards all who deviate from this absolute norm. In philosophy, we have the example of the Hegelian philosophy which identified the real with the rational and sought to justify the Prussian
state of its day as the embodiment of absolute values. Similarly,
Marxism, which is an inverted Hegelianism, involves the myth that
only the Communist state embodies all the social virtues and that
only the proletarian class is fit to represent mankind. What is particularly noteworthy in the case of the "Soviet myth" is that here
the identification of the absolute ideal with the political real was
undertaken in the name of a particular party and state, as well as
in the alleged interests of mankind as a whole. Mankind is divided
into two camps, the enlightened and the saved by the Grace of
Marxism, and the deluded and the damned by the original sin of
capitalism and idealism. There is no more tragic example in the
whole of human history than this mythological identification of
the absolute ideal and the historically real — a myth which has
split the world asunder into hostile blocs.

Historically, it may be shown that there have been various types
of cultural absolutism. *Relative ethnocentric absolutism* is the most
common. This is a naive absolutism in which one's own culture
is uncritically preferred to all others. Second, there is *classical his-*

12. *Theoretical Anthropology*, pp. 416-29.

torical absolutism, the notion that a particular epoch marked the summit of human achievement. This is the absolutism of the past and is identified with some golden age either in remote, mythological times or in some particular historical epoch such as "the glory that was Greece" or the medieval synthesis of the thirteenth century. Thirdly, there is *evolutionary, historical absolutism* which is oriented towards the future. This is a *serial absolute* which involves the notion that time and history inevitably make for cultural progress and that whatever is, is best for the time being. The nineteenth-century doctrine of evolutionary progress as an inevitable process, exemplified in Herbert Spencer, illustrates this notion. Fourthly, there is *millenial absolutism,* the doctrine that there is an end of history at some remote time in the future and that this will usher in an age of perfection and happiness for all mankind. This doctrine is linked with the belief in a Messianic Age in Hebrew and Christian theology. The Marxist philosophy of history combines elements of the evolutionary philosophy of progress together with a millennial age which will mark the end of the political state. Fifthly, *cultural relativism,* which is linked with cultural pluralism, involves what may be called *"relative absolutism"*; the idea that each culture system is autonomous and valid in itself and that cultural values are disparate but equal. The cultural relativist denies the validity of any absolute ideal of cultural progress but is prepared to regard each culture *as if* it represented an absolute system, even though the system is valid for its adherents only. Hence, it is claimed, each culture is worthy of tolerance by the adherents of other cultures. In practice, tolerance for other cultures is quite compatible with intolerance for "spontaneous variations" within a given culture in the interests of integration and social solidarity.

By contrast, the thesis I wish to maintain is that no historical culture is free from limitations and imperfections and that to identify the ideal with the historically given is bound to lead to falsification of the ideal absolute which may be approximated but never realized. On this assumption, free, constructive criticism and suggestions for reform are always in order, since one may point out the ever-present disparity between professed ideals and actual accomplishments with a view to bringing them into closer accord.

Otherwise, if one were complacently to accept the *status quo* of a given culture, one would be led to indulge in rationalization and mythical justification as the only means of reconciling the ideal and the actual, what ought to be with what actually prevails.

According to the position here maintained, the concept of an absolute value is a significant regulative norm. The absolute norm is real insofar as it is conceived as an ideal possibility whose validity is independent of its actual realization in a particular culture. Hence the ideal may serve as a goal of cultural endeavor which is radically different from the process, the going, whereby it is approximated. The moment this absolute norm is given expression within the context of a given culture, it becomes in part falsified. That is why every attempt to identify the ideal with the actually existent is a delusion, a myth which sets up a false idol and hinders cultural progress. The ideal absolute is compatible with cultural freedom and diversity, since it does not dictate categorically the particular form which all historical cultures must assume, but serves only as a regulative norm and measure by which to evaluate cultural expressions.

V

Finally, we turn to the problem of tolerance. We have seen that the cultural and moral relativist makes a virtue of tolerance because of his inability to find an acceptable criterion for measuring and comparing moral values as well as cultural progress in general. Not being a moral nihilist, he is prepared to treat each culture as if it were absolute or autonomous while recognizing its relative validity for a given society only. In practice, the attitude of the cultural relativists is one of cultural *laissez-faire* and mutual freedom of cultural life. The historic fact that there were states which adhered to an "ethics of violence" and to a philosophy of history which envisaged perpetual crises as inevitable did not enter into their peaceful perspective at all. They thought in terms of cultural compatibility and cultural harmony rather than in terms of cultural conflict and social revolution. It has taken the impact of the Second World War and the unending Cold War which has followed it to awaken some cultural anthropologists to the reality of cultural crises and to the need for cultural integration on a world scale.

The central epistemological problem is obviously the one of determining whether or not it is possible to find some criterion for comparing values and measuring progress. The underlying assumption of the cultural relativist appears to be that facts and values differ radically. Facts are thought to be objective and to exist independent of the observer. By contrast, values are regarded as subjective emotional preferences of individuals and societies and hence incapable of verification by the methods of science. That is why one can measure scientific progress and progress in technology but not in such humanistic spheres as philosophy, ethics and art.

At this point I find myself in agreement with John Dewey and maintain with him that the dichotomy of facts and values is not a valid or fruitful one. So-called facts are really truth-values, our human evaluations as to the truth of our ideas and experiences concerning the order of nature. Facts depend on judgments as to what is the case and may change with the attempt to verify these judgments in practice.[13] This is demonstrated by the history of science and by the constant revaluations of "facts."

Moral values are not different in principle from truth-values or scientific facts. Judgments of moral values are, in part, judgments about facts concerning the conditions and results of experienced objects; "judgments about that which should regulate the formation of our desires, affections and enjoyments."[14] Judgments of moral values are judgments as to what is *desirable* under given circumstances and provide a direction of conduct in regulating our desires. That is why moralists from the time of Aristotle have found it necessary to differentiate sharply that "good" which is the object of desire from the "true good" which is the object of deliberation and moral choice. Judgments of value are not, as Dewey has pointed out, separable from experience and nature and are therefore subject to verification by the consequences to which they lead. Reason and experience provide us with a criterion of truth in the

13. *Theoretical Anthropology,* p. 415.
14. John Dewey, *The Quest for Certainty,* p. 265.

sphere of ethics comparable in principle to truth in the realm of the natural and social sciences.

The moral life may be defined as the pursuit of happiness mediated by the cultivation of human excellence. A rational ethics is a normative discipline concerned with the critical evaluation of man's potentialities or functions with a view to promoting a life of virtue or excellence. While each virtue represents an absolute norm perfect in its kind, the acts by which it is realized are always relative to the requirements of the situation which confronts the individual and to the means available to him. The life of virtue, as Aristotle first understood, is a blend of absolute principles and relative means and can be evaluated properly only by a person of practical wisdom and experience. Not all men but only the wise man is the measure of virtue and vice, good and evil.

As suggested earlier, the principle of the biological relativity of ethics implies that ethical principles are valid for man as man and presupposes that there is a universal human nature which may be studied objectively by the methods of science. What is desirable for man, as distinct from what men happen to desire, may be established through norms of human excellence derived from reason and experience and the values so postulated will be absolute in the sense of having universal validity for all mankind. Absolute values represent "true goods" and are judgments as to what man ought to do in the regulation of his conduct.

What impresses me most in the comparative study of cultures is the fact of the universal assumption of absolute values in all cultures. In the ritual dramas of primitive cultures there is a symbolic re-enactment of the myths which tell how the original rites and institutions of the culture were introduced by the ancestors and gods and how the blessings foretold by them may be secured in the present. What is important is that the myths are believed and serve as an inspiration for public action and the conservation of the traditional *mores*. Primitive animism and polytheism make it easy for their adherents to accept ethnocentric, relative absolutes because each god or spirit prescribes his own rites and taboos which are valid for his "chosen" people. That is why primitive peoples tend to be tolerant of other ways of life on principle and do not expect members of other tribes and cultures to practice their special taboos and rituals. With the advent of monotheism, religious and ethical prescriptions become universalized absolutes valid for all men who are subjects of the one God. The universal God of monotheism tends to be a "jealous" God who tolerates no worship of other gods and other modes of conduct, a principle proclaimed most explicitly in the Decalogue of the Old Testament. As the God of Israel became also the one God of the Christians and Moslems, the persecutions and wars among the nations of the Western world increased as well owing in large measure to the intolerant faith and missionary zeal of their "pious" adherents. In the contemporary world the atheistic and militant faith of the Communists, with their myth of a classless world society under Soviet Russia's leadership, is in mortal conflict with the traditional religious faiths of both the East and the West for the conquest of men's souls.

Modern philosophy and science share with monotheistic religion a common faith in absolute truth and in objective, universal values. Science, it is now being realized, is not merely an instrument for gaining mastery over the forces of nature; it has also a normative, humanizing function in determining one's entire cultural perspective. As the rational and empirical pursuit of truth, science is an absolute value as well as a moral good. The use of scientific method for irrational purposes, such as the communication of myths, superstitions and prejudices, is a perversion of the spirit of science. There must be a will to truth, a willingness to acknowledge the absolute cross-cultural value of scientific truth and to utilize it for rational moral and aesthetic ends, if science is to serve to humanize mankind. It is the spirit of science, at once rational, progressive and self-corrective, which may serve as the norm of human culture as a whole, irrespective of its factual and technological achievements.

Normative science combines freedom and tolerance in the pursuit of truth with intolerance of falsity and of all those social movements which threaten freedom of the scientific enterprise. As the great humanists and scientists of the sixteenth and seventeenth centuries foresaw, freedom of thought in the pursuit of scientific and philosophic truth is a necessary condition of progress. But tolerance is not an absolute virtue; everything depends on the object of tolacerance. As Edmund W. Sinnott has pointed out, the spirit of science leads to a middle road between an intolerance based on static absolutism and a flabby tolerance based on indifference to truth-values and moral values.

Cultural relativism involves tolerance based on skepticism of universal, objective standards of value as well as denial of the idea of progress. As against this narrow interpretation of science in general and of cultural anthropology in particular, I have urged that a normative and humanistic interpretation of science leads one to integrate the scientific study of values and facts and to take the idea of progress in culture seriously. As Julian Huxley has indicated,[15] the idea of progress is significant in the evaluation of biological and cultural evolution and may be shown to have an objective basis in nature. The comparative study of cultures has made us conscious of the dangers of uncritical ethnocentrism but it has also provided us with the material and the incentive to transcend the limitations of relativism and ethnocentrism by the pursuit of normative truths capable of producing a universal, cultural unity based on a common core of rational values.

15. Julian Huxley, "Evolution, Cultural and Biological," in *New Bottles for New Wine*.

REFERENCES:

Benedict, Ruth. *Patterns of Culture,* Penguin Books, 1946.

Bidney, David. *Theoretical Anthropology,* Columbia University Press, 1953.

———— "The Philosophical Anthropology of Ernst Cassirer and its Significance in Relation to the History of Anthropological Thought" in *The Philosophy of Ernst Cassirer,* ed. P. A. Schilpp, Evanston, Illinois, 1949, 465-544.

Boas, Franz. *The Mind of Primitive Man,* MacMillan, 1938.

Dewey, John. *The Quest for Certainty,* Minton, Balch, 1929.

Durkheim, Émile. *The Rules of Sociological Method,* Chicago University Press, 1938.

Herskovits, Melville J. *Cultural Anthropology,* Knopf, 1955.

———— "Statement on Human Rights," in *American Anthropologist,* xlix (1947), 539-43.

———— "Some Further Comments on Cultural Relativism," in *American Anthropologist,* 60 (1958), 266-73.

Huxley, Julian. *New Bottles for New Wine,* Harper, 1957.

Kant, Immanuel. *Critique of Pure Reason,* tr. F. Max Müller, Mac-Millan, 1927.

Kroeber, A. L. and Clyde Kluckhohn. *Culture: A Critical Review of Concepts and Definition.* Papers of the Peabody Museum of American Archaeology and Ethnology, Harvard University Press, xlvii, no. 1, 1952.

Linton, Ralph. "Universal Ethical Principles: An Anthropological View," in *Moral Principles of Action,* ed. R. N. Anshen, Harper, 1952, 645-60.

Malinowski, Bronislaw. *Argonauts of the Western Pacific,* Routledge and Kegan Paul Ltd., 1922 and 1953.

———— *Coral Gardens and Their Magic,* George Allen & Unwin, 1935.

Nietzsche, Friedrich. *The Genealogy of Morals.* In *The Philosophy of Nietzsche,* Modern Library, 1937.

Spinoza, Benedict. *Tractatus Theologico-Politicus.* In *Chief Works of Spinoza,* tr. R. H. M. Elwes, Dover Publications, 1951.

Sumner, William Graham. *Folkways,* Ginn, 1940.

Tylor, E. B. *Primitive Culture,* 2 vols., London, 5th ed., 1913.

Chapter V

A Pattern for Relating Ethics and the Social Sciences

BY HERBERT JOHNSTON

As Professor James R. Brown pointed out in a recent article,[1] "What is needed is one or more organizations under whose auspices social scientists, philosophers, and theologians, both Catholic and Protestant, could meet and discuss public affairs from their own theological positions." I share Professor Brown's hope that "the Notre Dame meeting will be the beginning of a continuing series in pursuing the same inquiry," and am happy to have the opportunity of making some small contribution to it.

This paper[2] investigates the nature and relation of the social and the moral sciences from the point of view of the classic distinction between speculative and practical knowledge. The conclusion reached is one which I wish to present for your consideration rather than one which I should be prepared to defend with my life. Time permits only a skeletal outline of the position; perhaps subsequent discussion may allow some meat to be put on the bones.

Our first task is to find out what kind of knowledge is involved in the social and in the moral sciences. Before proceeding with this task, however, we should try to be as clear as possible about the meanings being attached to some of the terms used.

1. James R. Brown, "Theology and Public Policy Decisions," *Social Order,* VII, 7 (Sept., 1957), 296-303.
2. A portion of the paper is drawn from my article, "The Social and the Moral Sciences," *The Catholic Educational Review* (Oct., Nov., Dec., 1957). Reprinted by permission.

First, economics will be principally used as the example of the social sciences, not because it is the only or necessarily the best example, but because it is the one with which I happen to be least unfamiliar. For the same reason, ethics, or moral philosophy, will be used to exemplify the moral sciences.

Second, both the social and the moral disciplines will be called sciences in spite of contradictory views. Without at all pretending to reach definitively established conclusions so briefly, one may yet consider that the social disciplines can claim the name of science, though in a reduced or minor sense, because their conclusions reach a certain degree of universality. Those conclusions have a greater or less degree of applicability; they hold "for the most part." This is not at all the degree of universality or of necessity found in mathematics or even in the natural sciences; yet it is much more than the mere recording of singular facts or events. Gresham's law is not of the same nature as Boyle's law; but it can properly be called a law. Economics is not a science of the same nature as chemistry; but it can properly be called a science.

Likewise, the fact that moral philosophy is practical and normative, that it directs and prescribes actions, does not rule out its being a science. For ethics or moral philosophy is, after all, grounded in what is, in knowledge of reality. Ethics, then, is not based on emotion or on unconscious conditioning, and can also properly be called a science.

The relation of the social and moral sciences will depend on what kind of knowledge is involved in each. And probably the basic question at issue is whether they are speculative or practical sciences. The following outline of what is meant by speculative and by practical knowledge is based largely on the teaching of St. Thomas Aquinas and the commentary of Cardinal Cajetan on that teaching.

When we speak of the speculative and the practical intellect, St. Thomas points out, we are not speaking of two different powers, but of the same power looked at from different points of view. For it is accidental to that power which is the intellect that it be ordained or that it not be ordained to some operation. And it is this ordination, this direction, this purpose that distinguishes the speculative from the practical intellect. For the speculative intellect does not direct what it apprehends to any operation, but solely to the consideration of truth; whereas the practical intellect directs what it apprehends to an operation. The speculative and the practical intellect, then, differ according to the *end* involved; they remain, however, two aspects of one power.[3]

The speculative intellect seeks truth as its end; the practical intellect seeks truth as ordained to operation: to doing or making. And since the matter involved must be proportioned to the end, the subject matter of the practical sciences must be those things which can be done or made by our operations and the knowledge of which can be ordained to operation as its end, whereas the subject matter of the speculative sciences must be those things which are not done or made by our operations and the knowledge of which cannot be ordained to operation as its end.[4]

It will follow that some knowledge is speculative only, some is practical only, and some partakes of both orders. For knowledge can be called speculative in three ways. First, on the part of the things known, which are not operable (cannot be done or made) by the knower; for example, human knowledge of natural or divine things, things which cannot be made by men but must be known as they are given. Second, as to the mode of knowing; for example, a knowledge of a house obtained by defining and dividing and considering the universals predicated on it (the sort of knowledge which would enable one to describe a house and to say what it is, but which would not enable one to build a house); for this is to consider operable things in a speculative mode and not as they are operable. Third, as to the end; for the practical intellect ordains its knowledge to the end of operation, whereas the end of the speculative intellect is the consideration of truth. Therefore knowledge which is speculative by reason of the thing known is speculative only; but that which is speculative either according to its mode or according to its end is in one respect speculative and in another respect practical.[5]

3. St. Thomas Aquinas, *Summa Theologiae*, I, 79, 11, c.

4. St. Thomas, *In Librum Boetii De Trinitate*, V, 1, c. Cf. *In II Metaph.*, lect. 2, Cathala ed. No. 290; *In III De Anima*, lect. 15, Pirotta ed. No. 820. For an enlightening commentary on these passages, see Yves Simon, *Critique de la Connaissance Morale*, Declée, Brouwer, 1934, pp. 9-11, 61-63, 68, 72-73.

5. St. Thomas, *Summa Theologiae*, I, 14, 16, c.

Two comments should be made on this text. The first is that, as we shall see at greater length below, all knowledge, even that which partakes in some measure of both the speculative and the practical orders, can be reduced ultimately to one or the other; all knowledge is in the long run either speculative or practical.

The second is the point that Cardinal Cajetan makes in his commentary on the text paraphrased above, the distinction between the end of the knower and the end of the knowledge. If a builder, for example, considers how to build a house but does not on this occasion intend to put his knowledge into practice, his knowledge may be said to be speculative from its end on the part of the knower only, not on the part of the knowledge itself. For the knowledge of how to build a house is practical in itself, whether or not any particular person intends to put that knowledge to use.[6] The intention of the knower is accidental to the knowledge itself. Mathematics, for example, is of its very nature speculative knowledge of what is, even though the personal intention or end of someone who studies it may be to keep books or to build bridges. Metaphysics is, as knowledge, speculative, even though some people earn a living by teaching it. And moral science is practical in itself, because its conclusions are directive of human actions, even though a particular student of moral science may have no intention of guiding his own life by it. In this paper we are concerned with discovering the relations among various sciences, and hence with the *finis scientiae,* the end of the knowledge, not with the *finis scientis,* the end of the knower. This distinction is a basic one.[7]

On the basis of this explanation, it should be possible to distinguish four types of knowledge, the first two of which can be reduced to speculative knowledge and the last two to practical knowledge. The second and the third types will be especially relevant to our problem.

First, there is purely speculative knowledge, that of a non-operable object, that is, of something that we cannot do or make. This type of knowledge yields conclusions whose copula is *is* or *will be.*[8]

---

6. *Comm.* Card. Caiet. in I, 14, 16, parag. III (See Leonine edition of *Opera Omnia* of St. Thomas Aquinas).

7. Cf. *Comm.* Card. Caiet. in I, 79, 11, parag. II.

8. It is important to observe that a conclusion whose copula is *will be,* that

Such knowledge is not of itself directed to any further end. Examples of this type of knowledge would be the sciences of mathematics and metaphysics.

Second, there is speculative knowledge of an operable object, of something that we can do or make. In spite of its object, this knowledge remains speculative in its mode and its end, and is ultimately to be characterized as speculative rather than as practical knowledge. This type of knowledge also yields conclusions whose copula is *is* or *will be*. St. Thomas's example is the study of a house in order to obtain a descriptive definition of it as opposed to the (practical) study of a house as an architect studies it, that is, in order to know how a house *is to be* built. In this paper it will be maintained that the social sciences, taken in themselves and so far as they are autonomous sciences, fall within this category of knowledge and constitute speculative knowledge of an operable object; namely, the actions of men in the institution and operation, or the establishment and preservation, of human societies.

Third, there is remotely practical knowledge, that is, knowledge of an operable object for the purpose of remotely directing operation. This type of knowledge yields conclusions whose copula is *is to be, should be,* or *ought to be* done, and is ultimately to be characterized as practical rather than as speculative knowledge. Its speculative and scientific element comes from the fact that its conclusions are applied to objects that are in some degree universal, as moral science concludes to the rightness or wrongness of species or types or kinds of acts, not to the rightness or wrongness of individual acts. In this paper it will be maintained that when the social sciences are incorporated into the wider context of moral science they fall within this category of knowledge, that they then constitute practical knowledge and become practical science.

Fourth, there is purely practical knowledge. This is knowledge of an operable object for the purpose of immediately directing op-

---

is, a predictive conclusion, is not by that fact a practical conclusion. The difference between *is* and *will be* as the coupla of a conclusion is merely a difference in tense. The statement is still a statement describing a fact, not a statement prescribing what *is to be* or *should be* or *ought to be* done or made. It is this latter type of copula that marks the conclusion in which it occurs as practical.

eration; further, this type of knowledge applies its conclusions to action. These conclusions, of course, are in terms of what *is to be done*, and are applied to singular actions considered here and now. The example of this type of practical knowledge is prudence. There is, of course, no science involved here.[9]

Where do the social and the moral sciences fit into this schema? As already indicated, moral science falls within the third classification as remotely practical knowledge. Its conclusions — for example, "Lying is a type of act that is not in conformity with man's rational nature, and hence evil, and hence not *to be done"* — are only *remotely* practical because they deal with a *type* of act, with action taken universally. But they remain *essentially* practical because they are of their very nature directive of action.[10]

It is true that the type of knowledge characteristic of most of the *Nicomachean Ethics* and of the Prima Secundae of the *Summa Theologiae,* the science that we usually call general ethics and that we teach under that name, is practical only because of its ordination to the type of knowledge characteristic of the Secunda Secundae of the *Summa Theologiae,* the science that we usually call special ethics and that we teach under that name.[11] Taken alone,

9. Cf. Brother Edmund Dolan, "Resolution and Composition," *Laval Théologique et Philosophique,* VI (1950), 9-62, especially p. 17, n. 2. Perhaps the following schema will make the distinctions somewhat easier to keep in mind:

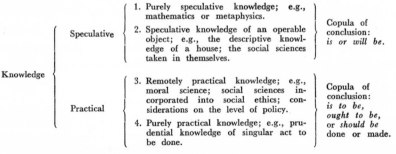

10. St. Thomas, *In I Ethic.,* lect. 3, Spiazzi ed., No. 40; *ibid.,* lect. 1, No. 1-2; *Summa Theologiae,* I,79, 11, ad 1. Cf. Yves Simon, *op. cit.,* pp. 78, 91-93, 103.

11. It is an indictment of our usual teaching methods, and perhaps an indication of mental confusion on our part, that we tell our students that their course in general ethics is the study of a practical discipline and then teach it

without such an ordination and outside of such a context, this knowledge would be psychology and metaphysics, both of them speculative disciplines. But in its context, such knowledge, even though its conclusions are in terms of what *is* rather than in terms of what *is to be* done, constitutes the introductory part of moral philosophy, of remotely practical knowledge. This is because the establishment of the end of man, the analysis of the human acts which are the means to that end, the further investigation of those acts in the virtues which are their internal principles and in law which is their external principle, constitute in their sum total a speculatively practical science ordained remotely to the direction of those human acts to that last end. Becoming less speculative and scientific and more practical as it approaches the singular, this same moral science yields conclusions in terms of what *is to be* done (as in the Secunda Secundae). As long, however, as it reaches conclusions of some degree of universality, it remains science. We are not in the realm of prudence until we reach a conclusion directing this individual action here and now, and the application of this conclusion, which is conscience, to that action.

St. Thomas provides a parallel in his description of medicine as a practical discipline. Following Avicenna, he sees medicine as practical when it is taken as a whole because it is ordained to the operation of healing. Yet this discipline contains, he points out, both a theoretical and a practical part. Its theoretical part would, for example, enumerate the kinds of fever; its practical part would direct that certain remedies should be applied to certain kinds of abscess. Because of its practical context, even the theoretical part of medicine should be classified as practical knowledge in spite of

---

to them in a purely speculative manner. Students can hardly be expected to see that what is taught to them as if it were psychology and metaphysics is a practical science if it is not hooked up in their course with the practical considerations to which it is supposed to lead. A two-semester course in ethics that includes both general and special ethics avoids this difficulty. But a one-semester course in general ethics is a pedagogical fraud when it masquerades as a practical science. Ethics could be taught as the practical science which it is even in one semester, but a good deal of revision of the traditional course would be necessary. This, however, would be the subject of another paper, and even of a new textbook.

the fact that, taken strictly in itself and outside of its inclusion in medicine, its conclusions are of a speculative nature.[12]

In more modern terms, this example would point out that the sciences studied in a present-day medical school, such as anatomy and physiology, could be considered practical disciplines because of their inclusion in medicine taken as a whole, even though in themselves they lead to conclusions of a speculative nature. In view of what follows, perhaps physiology would be an especially appropriate example. It studies an operable subject, the functions and vital processes of living organisms. Taken in itself and as an autonomous discipline, it studies them in a speculative mode or manner, and thus would fall within the second of the divisions of knowledge outlined above. In its context, however, considered as a part of medicine, physiology would fall within the third of those divisions and would become remotely practical knowledge. It is our contention that the same is true of the social sciences in relation to social ethics.

Before examining the social sciences to see into which division of knowledge they fall, there are two not uncommon extremes to be mentioned and avoided. The first is the positivistic doctrine that denies the name of science to practical, normative judgments, and that reduces conclusions about what ought to be done to mere personal preferences or childhood conditioning. In such a doctrine morals are a product of the society in which they exist, and change with the changing mores of that society. The social sciences, thus viewed, must imitate the methods of the natural sciences; they must, then, be purely speculative disciplines, and can have no subordination to moral philosophy, which latter discipline, in this view, does not exist as a science.[13]

The second and opposite error is that of holding that any discipline dealing with human action must, by that very fact, be a

12. *In Librum Boetii De Trinitate,* V, 1, ad 4. Cf. Yves Simon, *op. cit.,* pp. 51-54.

13. Though positivism among social scientists is no longer the unquestioned dogma it once was, it still has its devotees. See, for example, George A. Lundberg, *Foundations of Sociology,* Macmillan, 1939, pp. 27-31; Lundberg, *Social Research,* 2d ed., Longmans, Green, 1942, pp. 52-54; Arnold W. Green, *Sociology,* McGraw-Hill, 1952, pp. 2-9. Earlier examples, especially from Durkheim and Lévy-Bruhl, are quoted in Simon Deploige, *The Conflict Between Ethics and Sociology,* trans. Charles C. Miltner, Herder, 1938, pp. 90-92.

practical and normative discipline, despite the example of such sciences as psychology. This doctrine characterizes as positivism or scientism any hint of a value-free, morally neutral social science. It is unfortunately true that the assertion of the existence of such a value-free social science has, historically, often been accompanied by positivism, by the denial that any practical science either does or can exist. Yet the two positions are separable; one could logically support the former position while rejecting the latter one. It is at least possible, then (and is the position being maintained in this paper as true), that there could be a speculative study of social realities, in itself avoiding any value judgments, and yet in no way denying the existence or the necessity of a practical, moral science to which such a social science would be subordinate.

One error holds that there cannot be a practical science of human action; the other holds that there cannot be anything else.

The truth, this paper is maintaining, lies between these extremes. Economics and sociology and politics and anthropology are like the psychology contained in the Prima Secundae of the *Summa Theologiae* or like physiology and the other biological disciplines in the theoretical part of medicine. Taken in isolation they provide speculative knowledge of an operable object, and thus fall within the second of the types of knowledge outlined above. But taken in a practical context, included in that part of moral philosophy called social ethics, they provide remotely practical knowledge, and thus fall within the third of the types of knowledge outlined above. In such a context, the social sciences are directed to the attainment of a common good, to the establishment and preservation of one or another kind of temporal society.

In the same way the psychology of the Prima Secundae becomes ethics when it is incorporated into the essentially practical study of the human acts by which men may reach their end. And if the ethics is to be good ethics, really capable of guiding human life, the psychology had better be good psychology, pursued as the speculative study of an operable object. Physiology, again, becomes medicine when it is incorporated into the essentially practical study of the means of preventing and curing disease and preserving health. And if the medicine is to be good medicine, really capable of improving health, the physiology must be good physiology, pursued as the speculative study of an operable object. Finally, and this is our point, the social sciences become social ethics when incorporated into the essentially practical study of how to establish and preserve those societies in which men may best live fully human lives. And once more, if the social ethics is to be good social ethics, really capable of establishing and preserving those societies, the social sciences will first have to be sound in themselves, pursued, again, as the speculative study of an operable object and leading to value-free, ethically neutral conclusions.

The basic reason for this shift from the second to the third classification of knowledge is that the conclusions of these speculative sciences, from being simply objects of knowledge *known* as such, become, in a new context, means and intermediate ends *intended* as such, and thus pass into the practical realm. When considered practically in ethics, a certain virtue, for example, is no longer merely something described but something to be cultivated, that is, an end; but something to be cultivated in view of the further end of the good moral life, that is, a means — in summary, an intermediate end. When considered practically in medicine, a certain functioning of glands is no longer merely something described but something to be achieved as contributing, in turn, to the bodily health of the person. When considered practically in social ethics, a certain relationship of labor and capital is no longer merely something described but something to be pursued as contributing, in turn, to the health of society at large. But before such practical consideration, before such incorporation into a practical context through their results being intended and hence made means and intermediate ends, the observation and description in question remain on the level of objects of knowledge alone which are only potentially means, and hence constitute speculative knowledge.

In order to see whether this position holds up, let us briefly examine economics as an example of social science. In actual operation, economics seems to lead to two types of distinguishable but related knowledge. The first is description and analysis;[14] the

14. The laws arrived at in economic analysis do not, of course, pretend to the invariability of physical laws, but claim only some degree of generality. Among other factors, the existence of free choice in the persons whose behavior is observed and generalized makes impossible any physical necessity in economic laws. It does not, however, make impossible a high degree of psychological

second is prediction, which can become a hypothetical directive of action.[15] Description and analysis could be called pure economics; prediction and direction could be called applied economics. It is being held here that the subject matter and the conclusions of both pure and applied economics, taken in themselves, constitute the speculative knowledge of an operable object, that is, of certain kinds of human action, and fall within the second division of knowledge; taken in a practical context, however, they become incorporated into social ethics, constitute remotely practical knowledge, and fall within the third division of knowledge.

In the Introduction to his recent work, *Sociology,* Father Fichter speaks of the sociologist as sincerely trying "to avoid moral judgments."[16] I hope that he would not disagree with my seeing in this description an example of sociology taken as the speculative consideration of an operable object. On the other hand, Professor Boulding has recently characterized the function of economics as that of "The Taming of Mammon."[17] I should consider this view an example of economics taken as remotely practical knowledge and as a part of social ethics. Both aspects seem to be under consideration in the statement of the Postwar Program of the American Political Science Association of 1947, quoted at the beginning of the 15th chapter of Professor Wilson's *The American Political Mind.*[18] The same may, I believe, be said of Professor Bidney's

---

probability in economic laws, the only kind of universality being claimed for the conclusions of the social sciences, but a sufficient degree of universality to allow them properly to be called sciences. It is true, as Sidney Schoeffler points out in *The Failures of Economics,* Harvard University Press, 1955, that economics cannot claim to be a strict empirical science reaching invariable laws, for the basic reason that economists must artificially isolate their data to study them. Yet this fact does not establish the author's conclusion that economics is not a science, but merely that it is not a science in exactly the same sense that physics is a science. Still less does it establish his further conclusion that economics is an art.

15. Some of the difficulties involved in passing from analysis to prediction are pointed out by George Katona in "Expectations and Decisions in Economic Behavior," *The Policy Sciences,* ed. Daniel Lerner and Harold D. Lasswell, Stanford University Press, 1951, pp. 219-232.

16. Joseph H. Fichter, *Sociology,* Chicago University Press, 1957, pp. 7-8.

17. Kenneth E. Boulding, "Economics: The Taming of Mammon," *Frontiers of Knowledge in the Study of Man,* ed. Lynn White, Jr., Harper, 1956, pp. 132-149.

18. Francis Graham Wilson, *The American Political Mind,* McGraw-Hill, 1949, p. 404.

position in "The Concept of Value in Modern Anthropology." [19] An example may make this position clearer.

One of the areas of economic study is economic theory or general economics. On the macroeconomic level, which studies the whole economic system, efforts are made to predict more or less accurately the size of the national income from a study of private and public investment intentions. From the experience of previous years, the economist might have reached the conclusion that "an annual capital investment of so many dollars, other factors remaining equal, *does* maintain national income at such a figure." This generalization arose from observation and holds, obviously, only for the most part. This is an example of the first function of economics — analysis, or pure economics. The conclusion or law falls within the second division of knowledge, and constitutes speculative knowledge of an operable object. The second function of economics — prediction, or applied economics — would be based on this conclusion, and would be formulated somewhat as follows: "If annual capital investment is so much, then, other things being equal, national income *will be* maintained at such a level." Again, we have speculative knowledge of an operable object; the only thing changed is the tense of the copula of the conclusion. Finally, and as a continuation of applied economics, the prediction could be expressed as a *hypothetical* directive of action: "*If* you want to maintain national income at such a level, then, among other things, you *should* pass these fiscal laws encouraging investment."

In spite of the "should," the statement remains speculative, for the practical directive of action is only hypothetical. The economist has not made a statement about an end or a good or a value. He has supplied knowledge which, along with much other such knowledge, can be used as a means of reaching an end which has been decided on by someone else, an end about which, taken precisely as economic theorist, he has said nothing.

The transition from the speculative to the practical order occurs when this purely hypothetical directive loses its hypothetical char-

19. David Bidney, "The Concept of Value in Modern Anthropology," *Anthropology Today,* ed. A. L. Kroeber, Chicago University Press, 1953, pp. 682-698.

acter and becomes incorporated in a judgment in the area of social ethics, an area which runs from the most general normative judgments about society to the policy statements just above the prudential level. In this area, the conclusion in question would be stated as a policy directive, for example: "This government's fiscal policy should encourage investment." Finally, on the level of practice, which is the prudential level of the individual act to be done, a particular legislator would decide, "I should vote for this tax measure here and now proposed."

One final point. The position here being maintained would be opposed, not only by a positivist, but also, though for very different reasons, by one who agrees with David Easton, who says, "The ideal of a value-free social science has revealed itself as a chimera." [20] The reason that Easton gives for this conclusion is that social scientists themselves hold value premises that direct their attention to morally relevant problems in their field.[21]

It is certainly true that social scientists are men, and hence cannot avoid having value preferences. But this fact refers to what we have called above the *finis scientis,* the end of the knower, rather than to the *finis scientiae,* the end of the knowledge taken in itself. And our concern is with the kind of knowledge that social science constitutes, not with the moral convictions of social scientists. It is true and it is important that the moral convictions of social scientists about what ought to be, may be and perhaps usually are the things that direct their investigations along certain paths. If these moral convictions are more than personal preferences based on whim or prejudice or something equally unreasoned, if they are genuine conclusions based on considerations of the nature of man and of human society, then the whole enterprise, including the observation and analysis, has become a part of that practical science which is moral philosophy, and, more particularly, social ethics. But it does not follow that a value-free social science, taken in itself and outside such a practical context, is a chimera. For moral convictions have merely suggested to the social scientist his field

20. David Easton, *The Political System,* Knopf, 1953, p. 225.
21. David Easton, "The Decline of Modern Political Theory," *The Journal of Politics,* XIII, 1 (Feb., 1951), 45. Cf. *The Political System,* p. 223.

of investigation; they have not at all determined his findings. Moral science determines what ought to be, the end; social science determines what are the existing conditions out of which means to that end may be chosen and their feasibility *if* they are chosen as means. The first is practical; the second, taken in itself as an autonomous discipline, though one related to social ethics, is speculative. The failure of many social scientists and moral philosophers to make the distinction in practice does not alter its validity. Personal philosophical convictions on the part of the social scientist are important as well as inevitable; but they are not a part of social science taken in and by itself.

Those who maintain the practical nature of the social sciences and who say that these are *intrinsically* engaged in the wider practical context of social ethics, would presumably consider them parallel to what is usually called general ethics. But the reason why general ethics can be considered a practical science is that it includes the discovering of the end *to be pursued* as well as of the means of pursuing it. The social sciences, however, do not do this. It belongs to moral philosophy to establish the social end to be pursued; the social sciences are concerned only with the facts and their suitability as hypothetical means. They are, then, parallel to physiology rather than to general ethics. In themselves, they constitute the speculative consideration of an operable object, an example of the second classification of knowledge. Physiology can be but is not necessarily incorporated into the practical discipline which is medicine. When it is so incorporated, it becomes a part of medicine and, hence, practical. But in itself it remains an autonomous, speculative discipline. The study of the functions and vital processes of living organisms is an operation which can be pursued independently of the study of that practical discipline which is medicine. When it is so pursued it is speculative; when it is not so pursued it is practical, a part of medicine. The study of the functions of various social groups is also an operation that can be pursued independently of social ethics. When it is so pursued it is speculative; when it is not so pursued it is practical, a part of social ethics.

At this stage we believe that the following diagram will help to simplify and clarify matters.

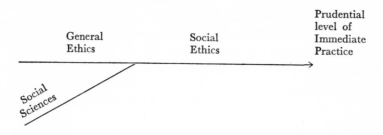

If I may be allowed, in Max Beerbohm's phrase, to sell my birthright for a pot of message, it is this: The making of social policy takes place in that part of the area of social ethics which is nearest to immediate practice. Lacking necessity and certainty, its conclusions yet try to express some faint degree of universality (perhaps "generalization" would be better) and to apply to a plurality of singular situations. The man skilled in general moral science should not try his hand at the making of social policy without undertaking a serious study of the facts of contemporary social life and of the social sciences. Casual observation is not enough to make an expert, and knowledge of the general does not guarantee knowledge of the more particular. Nor should the man skilled in the social sciences try his hand at the making of social policy without undertaking a serious study of the same facts of contemporary life (with which he is more likely to be already familiar) and of general moral science. For policy decisions are ultimately moral decisions; and both theology and moral philosophy are sciences that can be mastered only by study. Zeal for social justice and the regular practice of one's faith are not enough to make an expert, and knowledge of the social sciences as speculative does not guarantee knowledge of the social sciences as incorporated into that practical science which is social ethics.

Chapter VI

Inter-Disciplinary and Inter-Faith Dialogue as an Approach to the Study of Ethical Problems in Politics

BY JAMES R. BROWN

INTRODUCTION

The present time in the United States of America has been described by many as a period of renewed religious consciousness and
an era of reviving interest in the Christian Faith and its implications for social order. This religious revival has been called "The
New Look in American Piety,"[1] and serious questions are raised
as to the meaning of this phenomenon in American life.

This emphasis on the importance of religion raises an important
question: What is the relation of the theological convictions held
by individuals who are involved in forming public policy to the
decisions they must make? Unless the present concern over religion
is to be regarded as mere personal pietism, this question must be
raised and efforts made to explore at least the possibilities of discovering insights that will help us better understand the deeper
relationships between a man's religion and his public acts. The
question *has* been raised and the number of books and articles that
have been written about it give evidence that explorations towards
finding answers have indeed begun.[2]

1. *Christian Century,* Nov. 17, 1954, pp. 1395-1397.
2. Representative books on the problem:
   a. The search for a political theory: *Theory and Method in the Social
Sciences,* Arnold M. Rose, University of Minnesota Press, 1954. *The Political
System,* David Easton, Knopf, 1953. *Religion, Society and the Individual,*
J. Milton Yinger, Macmillan, 1957. *The Moral Foundations of Democracy,*

1. Definition of Terms

a. *The Meaning of Theological*

It is important to note that the question concerns "theological convictions." The term, theology, would include both dogmatic and moral theology.[3] Some of the important theological dogmas accepted by individuals that affect their decisions are the oneness of God, the Trinity, the person of Christ and His Mission, the Church and revealed religion.

The belief in God meant here does not necessarily demand an understanding of the treatise *De Deo Uno et Trino.* An individual may be said to believe in God when he regards God as the Creator and Ruler of the universe and particularly as the creator of each person's individual soul. This belief also frequently includes a conviction that man's final end is to be with God. It often extends to acknowledging that God has revealed to man, through the mission

---

John H. Hallowell, Chicago University Press, 1954. *The New Science of Politics,* Eric Voegelin, Chicago University Press, 1952.

b. The personalist solution: *You Can Change the World,* James Keller, Longmans, Green, 1948. *Government is Your Business,* James Keller, Doubleday, 1951. *Careers that Change the World,* James Keller, Doubleday, 1951. *Politics for Christians,* William Muehl, Association Press, 1956.

c. The social approach: *Christian Realism and Political Problems,* Reinhold Niebuhr, Scribner's, 1953. *Morals and Man in the Social Sciences,* J. V. Langmead Casserley, Longmans, Green, 1951. *Catholic Social Action,* John F. Cronin, Bruce, 1948. *Catholic Social Thought,* Melvin J. Williams, Ronald, 1950. *Christian Ethics and Moral Philosophy,* Geo. F. Thomas, Scribner's, 1955. *Christian Social Ethics,* Albert T. Rasmussen, Prentice-Hall, 1956.

d. Economic problems: *The Politics of Distribution,* Joseph C. Palamountain, Harvard University Press, 1955. *The Politics of Industry,* Walton Hamilton, Knopf, 1957. *Christianity and Economic Problems,* D. L. Munby, Macmillan, 1956. *Christian Values and Economic Life,* Bennett, Bowen, Brown and Osman, Harper, 1954.

3. Definitions: "Theologia definitur: Scientia quae, revelationis et rationis ope, disserit de Deo et creaturis quatenus ad Eum referuntur." Ad. Tanquery, *Synopsis Theologiae Dogmaticae,* 25th ed., Declée et Socii, 1945, v. 1, p. 2.

"Theologia est scientia eorum quae de Deo et de creaturis, ut ad Deum relatio, sunt demonstrabilia ex revelatione seu ex principiis fide creditis — scientia de divinis revelatis scientia et revelatione." J. M. Herve, *Manuale Theologiae Dogmaticae,* Berche et Pagis, 1952, v. 1, p. 2.

"Theology may be briefly described as the science of revealed truth." Geo. D. Smith, *The Teaching of the Catholic Church,* Macmillan, 1955, v. 1, p. 35.

of Christ and the prophets, as recorded in the Old and New Testaments and as taught by the Church, requisite knowledge of Himself and of the manner in which men are to live in order to attain their proper final end.

For the purposes of this discussion, belief in Christ includes His Incarnation, the Redemption and His Second Coming as the final judge of the human race. It involves faith in the power of sanctifying grace as the means by which the Redemption takes effect in the souls of men. This belief in Christ as the Son of God makes His life, death and resurrection the most important events in human history since the beginning of time and to the end of the world.

The general concept of the Church as an object of general belief embraces the whole corporate and individual spiritual life of man. The Church is regarded as the normal channel of grace and the witness to the truths of the Gospel to the end of time within whose community and by whose aid men work out their eternal salvation. The Church is regarded by many believers as the fellowship of the faithful or the mystical Body of Christ on earth in time.

Moral theological ideas included in the phrase "theological convictions" as used in the statement of the problem are a recognition of the Divine Law and the obligations that it imposes upon men; man's sinfulness before God and the effects of sin in the lives of men; grace as the remedy for sinfulness and its application to the souls of men through the prayer of faith and the relation of the Christian natural law to the Divine law of God and the positive laws of men.

In this presentation "theological convictions" means belief in the basic dogmatic and moral teachings of the Christian religion as found in the traditional Symbols of the Church. It is not concomitant with the Catholic Faith since it is not as broad in its extension as the tenets of that Faith, but it does mean traditional Christianity excluding all systems of belief which depart radically from the Christian articles of faith.

Let it be noted here that this is a self-imposed limitation. It does not mean that theological convictions are limited to Christian theological convictions and that others do not count or are not important on the American scene. It does mean that this paper is limited to a consideration of the relationship between traditional Christian theological convictions and public policy making.

b. *The Meaning of "Public Policy Making"*

The phrase "public policy making" covers all decisions which have public effect. This, of course, means decisions of elected officials which are made in the performance of their office whether they be executives, legislators or judges. It also means the decisions of elected party officials especially those concerned with the nomination of candidates for public office at all levels in the party structure.

Public policy making likewise embraces those decisions of business and professional men which are in the area of public affairs. In effect this includes most of the big decisions concerning the operations of the larger business institutions in the United States. It also includes decisions made by professional and trade associations that result in pressure group activities and lobbying. Thus when U. S. Steel announced on December 27, 1950, that it would build history's largest single steel expansion project, the $400 million Fairless Works at Fleetwing, N. J., near the Delaware River, which resulted in the creation of a new Levittown, in Bucks County, Pennsylvania, it made public policy. So did the National Education Association when it voted its approval of federal aid to education and its opposition to the use of public funds for parochial schools, at its annual meeting in St. Louis, Missouri, July 2-7, 1950.

However, policy is made by others than the few. Public policy making extends to the electorate when they participate in the selection of candidates for public office. The voter is participating in public policy formation when he goes to the polls and casts his vote for one candidate or the other. He indirectly participates in that process insofar as policies are shaped with regard to the possible reaction of the electorate in a future election. This means, of course, that public policy making goes on concurrently at several levels. It is not just the private preserve of the few who are well known because of their positions in public or private life.

The relation of the theological convictions of individuals to public policy making is a broad and complex problem, yet one which exists within some discernible limits. It has what might be called positive and negative aspects. The positive aspect is the effect of actual theological beliefs held by a person upon real concrete decisions that he must make or that he tries to avoid. The negative aspect is the effect of beliefs so broad and so unclear as to amount to no convictions at all, upon an individual's decision-making process. We are concerned with the positive aspect only in the course of these remarks, although it is recognized that lack of "confessional" theological convictions has very pronounced effects on policy formation.

c. *Three Basic Concepts Commonly Used in Discussing the Problem*

(1) THE COMMON GOOD

The common good is that which is supposed to be realized by all proper political action. It is the announced objective of any politician asking for the support of a large electorate. However, the articulation of this good, the realization of it in specific instances is fraught with serious political conflicts and severe tensions. The goal of the common good is reached only by great effort, many compromises and deep disappointments.

Most of the weekly news magazines in this country have concerned themselves with the problem of the present inflationary trend in our economy and all of them have stated that the trend ought to be checked — for the common good. The classic approach had been to restrict the amount of money by raising interest rates and to reduce government expenses while maintaining taxes to pay off the debt. A more recent solution has been to ask the leaders of business and labor to "have the responsibility to reach agreements on wages and other labor benefits that are fair to the rest of the community as well as to those persons immediately involved. . .[negotiated raises] should be consistent with productivity prospects and with maintenance of a stable dollar. And business must recognize the broad public interest."[3a] In addition the Presi-

3a. *Annual Economic Report,* Jan. 23, 1957, reported in *Facts on File,* Jan. 17-23, 1957, p. 28.

dent asked consumers to voluntarily curb their purchasing in this period of rising prices.[4] The common good is the same — halting inflation and maintaining a high level of employment, but it is not crystal clear which is the best way to articulate it.

Within the Church the concept of the common good [5] is also regarded as the proper goal for political institutions to strive for when carrying out their assigned functions. However, the articulation of that concept in a given socio-economic situation at a specific time and place is not so clear.

The manner in which the great social encyclicals are implemented illustrates the difficulties. Most good Catholics say they agree with the principles of the encyclicals,

> . . . but once you present them with a given principle in the concrete — a program, policy or law — they cry out: New Dealish, socialistic or worse. . . . (*America,* Aug. 17, 1957, p. 597.)

Since the conflict within the Church over the meaning of the common good in specific instances is widely known, it is not diffi-

---

4. News conference Wed., Oct. 30, 1957.

5. "[The common good] is an end constituted by the assurance of the necessities of life to the subjects [of the state], by the establishment of internal harmony through the just distribution of rewards and penalties and by giving security against external enemies. The ultimate common good of the state has been summed up by Thomas and Aristotle as 'the life of virtue' or the life of reason for the whole community." Walter Farrell, *A Companion to the Summa,* v. II, Sheed and Ward, 1938, p. 369. Cf. St. Thomas, *Summa Theologica,* I-II, 90, a. 2.

"Bona proprie socialia, videlicet ipsam societatis constitutionem, formam regiminis, rerum publicarum administrationem, relationes inter varios civium ordines, necnon diffusionem totius communitatis jurium contra exterarum gentium injustam aggressionem." Ad. Tanquery, *Theologia Moralis Fundamentalis,* ed. by F. Ametier, 11th ed., Declée et Socii, 1945, v. II, p. 254.

"The good of society . . . the common good .. . is expressed in the words 'public peace and prosperity.' " Wm. F. Drummond, *Social Justice,* Bruce, 1955, p. 13.

"Hence it is the whole prerogative and function of the State to control, aid and direct the private and individual activities of national life that they may converge harmoniously toward the common good. That good can neither be defined according to arbitrary ideas nor can it accept for its standard primarily the material prosperity of society, but rather it should be defined according to the harmonious development and the natural perfection of man. It is for this perfection that society is designed by the Creator as a means." Pius XII, *Summi pontificatus,* Oct. 20, 1939; see Harry C. Koenig, *Principles for Peace,* National Catholic Welfare Conference, 1943, p. 606.

cult for Catholics to appreciate and understand this kind of conflict in the political order. Here they can see what the problem
of applying a political ethic means.

(2) TRUTH: AS THE BASIS OF POLITICAL JUDGMENT

In the realm of politics, best illustrated by the legislative process,
prudential judgments are made in the practical order as the result
of research and debate. The process of debate nearly always produces conflicts between men who interpret the same set of facts
differently. The final product comes out of the conflict and necessary compromise that the debate engenders, and it is usually different than that which would have been produced had any one of
the protagonists of the conflict had complete control of the situation.

Thus, for example, the production of a law such as the Employment Act of 1946 (60 Stat. 24; 15 U.S.C. 1023) involved such
giving and taking on the part of all those working for and against
the law that the result was different from anyone's original expectations. As it happens this law has worked rather well, probably
better than any of the original proposals would have turned out.
And the process of change goes on in response to the changes in
the politico-economic context of the law.

A question can be raised as to whether or not (1) the Church
articulates its response to the given situation — or (2) deduces the
response from unchanging principles, following the laws of logical
reasoning without reference to any external situation. The question is discussed in relation to the teacher's role when he is dealing
with Catholic thought by Father Andre Godin:

> Finally the teacher will never hesitate to indicate when he can
> that Catholic thought has not yet completed its elaboration of the
> treasure which has been confided to it. Some of its implications
> are still under seal and they will become accessible only slowly with
> the help of the Spirit which cannot fail it. If this is true even
> in the case of scientific knowledge as it penetrates the meaning and
> the forces of the material and psychic world, it is still truer in the
> case of the dogmas of Christianity, which have only begun to deliver
> up to men the impenetrable riches of the mystery of Christ in its
> relation to cosmic and psychological forces. . . .

He will point out that the laity has an irreplaceable role to play if the sacred deposit of doctrine which has been revealed to us centuries ago is to continue to develop and to produce its best fruits.[6]

For those Catholics who hold the second point of view, there are great difficulties in trying to understand the relation of theology and ethics to the dynamics of politics. For the others the road is not so thorny since they see a similar process at work within the Church itself.

(3) THE CONCEPT OF GOD IN RELATION TO MAN'S UNDERSTANDING

Policy makers who are strongly pietistic and who accent God's unchangeableness may, like President William McKinley, make policy on their knees as he did when ordering the liberation of the Philippines from the fetters of Spanish governmental and religious ideas.[7] More realistically a politician of principle understands his dependence upon God *and* the relevance of all true facts. He also recognizes the contingency of any political decision. He follows the dictum of St. Ignatius of Loyola, "To pray as though everything must come from God, and to act as though everything must come from ourselves. . ."

There is a great danger in the first point of view, as the mistakes of many a "righteous" politician amply illustrate. The second point of view, not losing sight of God's unchangeableness, but concentrating upon His relation to contingency, is more responsive to the becoming situation, as Abraham Lincoln, for example, was.

Within the Church the concept of God may accent His Immutability without remembering that God's changelessness implies that God *is* Act; He *is* Truth. The implications of all being in Him are self-known and eternally realized, and this includes the whole process of becoming and change.

For Catholics who look upon God as unchanging and somewhat outside history, there is, again, real difficulty in understanding how

6. "The Tensions of Catholicism," Andre Godin, *Thought*, Dec. 1950, pp. 645-46.
7. *Dictionary of American Biography*, vol. XII, p. 108.

His Truth can be related to the kaleidoscope of politics. But to those who look upon the Changeless God revealing Himself through the unfolding of the historical process, understood anew by the concrete individual personalities of each living generation, the relationship is more easily made.[8]

2. CAUSES OF THE PROBLEM

There are many political and economic reasons why the problem of theological convictions and public policy decisions is important today. The two actually always work together, as the old term "political economy" suggests. Separating one from the other

8. "Considered in creation—physical world and rational world—the work of God is the same cosmic and human process as existence, order and vitality dependent on God. This dependence on God, rationally translated into an idea, becomes a motive of human activity, not only as religious belief and worship but in all the intellectual and moral effects that this idea produces. Thus, we may truly say that the reflection of God in creation and in its laws, translated into idea, is historicized by means of human activities. . . . The divine in history cannot be denied. For us, it is the Absolute that creates the relative, and in order to make Itself known, communicates Itself to the relative and puts on humanity: and this is history, true history. The divine that becomes history, or historicizes itself, not only does not break the laws of human process, but may indeed be said to integrate them. The circle of Transcendence-Immanence and Immanence-Transcendence, which is the law of creation and of the cosmic destiny, can more easily be fulfilled by each man when through the historical manifestations of the divine, he wins the potentiality of being transformed in it." Don Luigi Sturzo, *Inner Laws of Society,* Kenedy and Sons, 1944, pp. xxxii-xxxiv.

"The very notion of development shatters any view of the finite as a closed order because it requires us to regard the finite as opened upward to an infinitely creative reality to which it is dynamically related. . . .

"Given a real development of concrete things, especially of man, we are compelled to eschew everything that savors of a static relation of the relative to the absolute, or which suggests a crudely dualistic relation of process to the Divine Thought. As against the ancient immobilism, our conception must be through and through a creationism, with a powerful accent on its infinite character, and a bringing forward the dynamic and life-giving tension that exists between every concrete thing and its Idea." Robert C. Pollock, "History is a Matrix," *Thought,* vol. 26 (Summer, 1951), pp. 216-217.

". . . . whereas in the past spiritual life tended to loosen man's connections with his universe, it now had the opposite effect, for the more he enters into commerce with God, the more vital is the need to overstep limitation and deficiency. Static truths and values become unendurable, for they have to be brought into life if there is to be growth toward infinity." Robert C. Pollock, "Freedom and History," *Thought,* vol. 27 (Winter, 1951), p. 413.

is an exercise in logical abstraction in order to observe them more closely, but it must always be remembered that they do not actually exist separately. The political causes which in their turn have contributed greatly to the raising of the problem of theology and politics may at this time be divided into international and domestic.

a. *International Political Causes*

The sustained attack of Communism against religion and free government throughout the world is one of the major international causes. Communism is more than just another form of government: it is a political theory which presents a materialistic solution to difficulties of decision making in today's world. The materialism of Communism, however, is presented in an idealistic manner and it does motivate men and women who are convinced members of the Party to make great sacrifices in order to bring about the establishment of the Communist society. Communism, then, is somewhat like a religion in its impact on the minds of men, and it demands answers which transcend mere positivistic pragmatism. As the celebrated exchange between Marshall Zhukhov and President Eisenhower suggests, mere appeals to quantitative factors do not really answer Communism.[9] Besides, the Communists may well duplicate our material accomplishments.

The work of the United Nations and the effects of its decisions throughout the world has also helped to raise the problem. The United Nations presents itself to the world as an organization which is motivated by high ideals and moral principles and in so doing it raises the question as to what those ideals and principles really are: Are they basically just materialistic and positivistic expediency clothed in moralistic terms? Or are they spiritual and teleological motives which flow from beliefs that are theological in origin?

The same question may be raised about the United States foreign

---

9. Presidential news conference, July 17, 1957. "We tried to explain to each other just what our systems meant . . . to the individual and I was very hard put to it when he insisted that their system appealed to the idealistic, and we completely to the materialistic and I had a very tough time trying to defend our position." *New York Times,* July 18, 1957.

policy, which is also presented to the world at home and abroad as a "good" policy [10] as over against the "bad" policy of our opponents in the game of diplomacy. Does our policy flow from and is it informed by theological convictions which are the product of our history and tradition or is it simply self-interest sweetened by the adjective "enlightened" with frequent references to justice, peace and human welfare? The attack of Communism, the operations of the United Nations and the formulation and implementation of our own foreign policy are contributory causes to the rise of the problem of the relation of theology to politics.

b. *Domestic Political Causes*

Questions of domestic politics likewise contribute to the raising of this problem. What concept of justice pervades the halls of legislatures and the offices of administrators? Is it one which is based upon the moral law or is it a product of pragmatism? What is the relation of private morality to public life? Does a man qualify as a good Catholic or a good Protestant simply because his personal moral and religious life are above reproach even though his public acts are open to serious question? What is the morality of political campaigning? Is it justifiable to exploit a candidate as a religious symbol of security just because campaign managers believe that people will be motivated to respond favorably to such symbols, even though there may be no real basis for either? These are domestic

---

10. "(The Constitution) sometimes seems to be cumbersome, but under it our country has grown from an infant to being perhaps the greatest country in the world—and I refer to greatness not only in terms of material power but in terms of our moral influence in the world." John Foster Dulles, U.S. Sec'y of State. "Economic and Military Cooperation with Nations in the General Area of the Middle East," Hearings before the House Committee on Foreign Affairs, 85th Cong., 1st Sess., Jan. 7, 1957, p. 51.

"Our world policy and our actions are dedicated to the achievement of peace with justice for all nations." Pres. Eisenhower, State of the Union, Jan. 5, 1956.

"We have no other interests to advance. We have no desire or intent to subjugate or subvert other peoples—no purpose to change their chosen political, economic, or cultural patterns—no wish to make any of them our satellites. We seek only to further the cause of freedom and independence and to develop the military strength necessary to protect and defend it, in the interest of peace." Pres. Eisenhower, For. Aid Program Message, March 19, 1956.

questions that are forcing men to become concerned about the true relation of theology to politics.

c. *Economic Causes*

There are economic difficulties that have theological implications. The present economy could be called an economy of abundance and the very words evoke pleasant pictures of the good life for everyone with comfortable homes, ample transportation, welfare for all and a host of gadgets. However, serious men and women are wondering about the moral and religious implications of such an economy. There are evidences that economic abundance produces more than the good life: the emphasis upon the acquisition and rapid use of more and more material goods may well be undermining the moral and spiritual fibre of the citizens of the country and questions are being raised about the relation of juvenile delinquency to this abundance. Furthermore, as Vance Packard demonstrates in *The Hidden Persuaders*,[11] there is a real question to be raised about the ethics of the advertising techniques and the use of motivational research data which are resorted to in order to stimulate the public to greater and greater consumption of material goods just to keep the economy expanding.

The unevenness of the distribution of the economic goods of the world causes severe tensions between the nations and regions of the world that are relatively depressed and those that are enjoying a high material standard of living. Tensions are also caused between different groups within U. S. society and within individuals who are trying desperately to raise their socio-economic status in order to gain prestige.

II. THEORY OF THE INSTITUTE

The Institute of Ethics and Politics at Wesleyan University is an organization attempting to acquire new and better insights into how theology affects policy formulation in the concrete individual and by this investigation perhaps make some contribution toward a

11. Vance Packard, *The Hidden Persuaders*. McKay, 1957.

better understanding of the decision-making process, particularly when moral elements are involved. In Catholic terms this would aid the work of the lay apostolate, and in Protestant terms narrow the gap between the pulpit and the pew. It is fully realized that such an answer will be found only after the work of many such groups as the Institute has been done for a number of years.

The Institute, as presently organized, consists of a group of social scientists of different faith commitments in the Public Affairs center of Wesleyan University at Middletown, Connecticut, and some theologians from the Yale Divinity School in New Haven. During its operations, however, men from other schools, such as Harvard Divinity School and Fordham University have participated in conferences. The Wesleyan faculty group has included at least one Catholic social scientist since shortly after the Institute's foundation, although it is admitted that the group has been predominantly Protestant in membership and orientation. This is more an accident of its location and its founders than a studied effort to keep Catholic participation to a minimum.

The theory underlying the Institute of Ethics and Politics is that public policy making takes place at all levels in our society, not just at the top, and that the responsibility for policy decisions is shared by many more than the well-known national leaders. Furthermore, public policy, in the United States, is formed in an inter-faith atmosphere and any attempt to understand the process must take place in a like atmosphere. Finally, the area of public policy is an area which touches upon all of the major disciplines of the social sciences, hence any endeavors on the part of the academicians to understand policy formulation must take place via an inter-disciplinary as well as an inter-faith approach.

1. The Pervasiveness of Policy Making

One rather popular error[12] prevalent in the United States today is that real policy is made only at the top. This leads to the abdica-

---

12. Shared by such men as James Burnham, *Managerial Revolution*, Putnam, 1943; H. D. Lasswell, *Politics, Who Gets What When, How*, McGraw-Hill, 1936.

tion of responsibility on the part of most citizens who believe that since policy is only made at the very top, and since the persons at that level making policy are far removed from the local scene, there is no reason to feel responsible for such policy. One result of this point of view is a willingness on the part of many to find a scape-goat for any errors made in policy making, thus leaving it possible for unscrupulous politicians to suggest that the failure of our China policy, for example, was entirely the fault of a few men in the State Department in the previous administration. The signs are not want-ing that a similar operation will shortly be launched against the present administration and the loss of American prestige in the Mid-dle East may be ascribed to President Eisenhower's failure to press for more funds for missile and rocket research in his budget mes-sages. This divorce of policy from responsibility raises a host of in-teresting questions about the democratic state that we cannot ex-amine here.[13]

Another result of this popular attitude is the failure to observe that state and local political party leaders, United States senators and representatives, governors, state legislators, mayors and council-men are all engaged in policy making, and a great many times in policies which for all their local application are conceived of in reference to the national scene and in relation to the long range results of such policies upon the communities themselves which can only be thought of in the context of state and federal policies. It overlooks the implications of these decisions and the fact that they touch the lives of most people in the community, not just in the present but for many years in the future. The decision to engage in slum clearance involves state-federal and state-city-federal rela-tions, the economy of the state and city involved, and the lives of the people directly and indirectly affected for many years to come.

When the activities of local and state officials are not regarded as policy making, a great deal of indifference exists about them. The statistics of local elections give ample witness to the existence of this indifference. This, in turn, produces two other unfortunate results. Public policy makers at these levels are at best often medi-ocre men or at worst simply dishonest men who make policy for

13. See Eric Voegelin, *The New Science of Politics,* Chicago University Press, 1952.

short time purposes only, without regard to the fact that what they are doing has the ramifications of which we speak. From the standpoint of the Institute's theory, public policy making can only be understood in the complex context of policy being made at all levels within the cultural milieu of the period in which any specific policy is formed.

2. THE INTER-FAITH ASPECTS OF PUBLIC POLICY MAKING

For years theology has been delegated to the periphery of academic institutions except those dedicated to the preparation of men for the priesthood or ministry. Among scholars, religion courses are commonly regarded as unimportant so far as any serious study is concerned, and among students they are traditionally known as "gut" or "snap" courses. It is exceedingly important for a proper investigation of public policy making that direct contact be restored between theology and the social sciences and that the latter come to recognize the role theology has of informing history, economics, political science, sociology and anthropology.

This is important on the academic or research level because theology does play a role in the work-a-day world. Hence, not only must theology be restored to its proper place among the academic disciplines, but in the work of the Institute it must come in through an inter-faith approach. The reality of the situation is that public policy in the United States is made in an inter-faith context. Although there are loud protestations that there is a "wall of separation" between the church and state in this country, only the naive are deceived by this, because the record clearly shows that church and state are not so separated as it seems. All that is necessary to demonstrate the truth of the proposition that public policy is formed in an inter-faith context is to propose a policy where the contact is direct. For example, any discussion of federal or state aid to schools quickly brings up the question as to whether private religious schools can qualify for this aid and once that question is raised the confessional position of the disputants begins to appear.

Most of the time, however, inter-faith differences do not become so sharp. The Institute theory of the necessity of the inter-faith approach is not only geared to the reality that public policy is made in an inter-faith context, but it is a recognition of the fact that men of different theological convictions can try to understand how they think about public policy from their different confessional positions without losing any of their religious identity. Most of the time this takes place at a very low level indeed, with the accent on "brother-hood" and "good fellowship" without any real effort to penetrate the "other fellow's" point of view. However, it has been demon-strated that men and women of different faiths can make successful efforts to view a problem from the position of another's faith com-mitments without losing or weakening their own. It has happened that men who disagree very much on a matter because of their different theological credos have become very rational and even sympathetic about that disagreement when they have made real efforts to try to understand a problem from the point of view of another faith than their own. And this can take place even where neither side condones that which is regarded as error and there is no immediate possibility of solution. When such efforts to under-stand are made, there is always clearer thinking than that which goes on when men of differing views merely try to present their own positions in a defensive manner and usually end up by talking about two or more different things.

In fact, the inter-faith atmosphere in which American public pol-icy is forged is one which does produce much more cooperative ac-tion than uncooperative friction, and this action is achieved by men of different faiths without the dilution of anyone's theological beliefs. And this is not to suggest that in these cases the parties act without religious motivation or that democratic action works only in the realm of materialism divorced from theology as T. V. Smith[14] avers. A housing development can be built without public refer-ence to religious reasons for such activity, but the participants in such a project often see themselves as acting within their own the-ological frameworks while engaged in the project. Thus a good Catholic may work in such a project because he believes it is a work of justice in the natural law sense, while a good Protestant may do so because he regards it as an expression of the social justice

14. Cf. *Promise of American Politics,* Oxford, 1936, and *Power and Con-science,* Free Press, 1950.

contained in the Beatitudes. The difference exists, but the cooperation continues.

The cooperative activity of men and women of different religious conviction means a recognition of the fact that tensions between religious groups must and do exist, and that harmony, i.e., agreement upon a set of religious beliefs so general in content as to be actually meaningless is not necessary for the establishment of deep understanding. Differences may continue to exist between men who can act together cooperatively. It is the contention of the Institute that where it is possible for a dialogue to take place while the specific cooperative activity is formulated and carried out, it may well produce new insights into reality that cannot come about in the absence of such dialogue.

3. THE INTER-DISCIPLINARY APPROACH

Even as public policy is made in an inter-faith atmosphere, it can only be adequately understood when it is seen in the context of the social sciences although it is recognized that policy may not be formally hammered out in such an academic climate. Actually each of the social sciences can gain new insights into its own body of knowledge by trying to understand itself in terms of and from the positions of the others. The view of political science that is entertained by a trained economist is something quite different from the political scientist's view of his own discipline. And although it is perfectly true that political scientists cannot easily become trained economists, it is not necessary that they do so in order to have a sympathetic understanding of the economist's point of view. The unfortunate thing is that such efforts are so seldom made. Most of the time either the economist or the political scientist is likely to regard the other as an interloper and make some unpleasant remarks about each sticking to the field in which he is competent.

And yet the attempt of one social scientist to understand his own discipline in the terms of other social sciences does not involve giving up a "private preserve" nor does it mean the dilution of either discipline. When the historian tries to understand history from the point of view of the sociologist, he is not losing anything to the sociologist nor is he the less of an historian because he has taken time out from his own studies to try to see them from the position of another social science. It is recognized that this cannot be genuinely done without two things: it is necessary that a group of social scientists do this on a continuing basis over a period of time long enough to establish a thoroughly friendly community and a real knowledge of each other as persons. It is also necessary that they listen, really listen, to each other and read attentively in each other's fields. The addition of theologians to such groups only properly rounds them out and adds a catalytic agent that otherwise might be lacking.

When social scientists begin to work together in the area of public policy making they are likely to engage in real inter-disciplinary understanding because this is one area upon which all social sciences necessarily touch and come into contact. The attempt to understand public policy making by such a group inevitably means entering into a process of cultural analysis and this, of course, cannot be adequately done by any of the social sciences alone. Sociology may be thought of as the particular social science that tried most to do this, yet a look at sociology as an attempt to understand the whole culture quickly reveals that history is necessary, the sociology of politics is involved, economic sociology enters into the analysis, and so forth. And this can only be most fruitfully done by a group of social scientists working in a disciplined way together, and at the same time within their own subject areas on the common problem.

4. THE METHODOLOGY OF THE INSTITUTE

The theory of the Institute was developed out of a faculty seminar and the succeeding work of the organization rather than from speculative thought of any kind. A faculty group of social scientists from the Public Affairs Center at Wesleyan met together for a scholastic year as a seminar studying the general topic of ethics and politics. The group was motivated by a desire to find a common ground for the study of public affairs by economists, historians and political scientists, but in the course of their reading and discussion they became more interested in theology and the impact of theological convictions on public policy making. Dr. Kenneth Underwood, professor of Christian social ethics at Yale Divinity School, chaired the seminar, and the social scientists read at length in the writing of leading Protestant theologians. For many professors this was their first contact with theological writing of any kind. One result of the seminar was the conclusion that theology should be brought into better contact with the social sciences and one of the purposes of founding the Institute was to achieve this result. The Institute itself continued the seminar as a mixed faculty-student course and engaged in conferences and depth interviews in the course of its development.

a. *The Mixed Seminar*

The mixed faculty-student seminar is offered as a Public Affairs course (Social Ethics and Public Policy) on some area of public policy making. Thus, one year the seminar was concerned with the theology that bears upon the decisions of a government to support economic abundance as a political policy — going beyond the assumption that it is simply a good vote-getting technique. The student members of the seminar are chosen from various major fields on the basis of the interest they expressed in a study of policy making and their intellectual aptitude for it. The faculty members are selected so that there are three members, one from each of the three departments (economics, history and government) always present. The chairman is a theologian and for the first two years a Catholic political scientist was a regular faculty participant. The number is small: 8 to 12 students and 4 to 5 faculty members.

The seminar usually spends its first weeks doing much reading in the writings of theologians and carrying on a vigorous discussion, where different positions are frankly stated, in order to get some theological background. Selections from such representative writers as Jacques Maritain, Reinhold Niebuhr, Albert T. Rasmussen, Martin Buber, Martin D'Arcy, Richard Niebuhr, John S. Cronin,

Paul Tillich, John Courtney Murray and Dietrich Bonhoeffer are read and discussed in relation to the central topic of the seminar.[15]

Having at least become acquainted with some of the theological writers whose works concern social questions, and having become aware of the implications of theological doctrines in social matters, the seminar reads and discusses the writings of social scientists pertinent to the course and discusses these in relation to the theological writings previously studied. During this part of the seminar, efforts are made to read in all the social sciences that have concerned themselves with the problem at hand.

Finally, the students write papers upon some aspect of the study being made in which they try to bring together the results of their inquiries and the effect of those inquiries upon their own theological positions. These papers are discussed at seminar meetings. The results of the seminar have been good. The faculty has been given an opportunity to learn more about the students' real points of view, and their own points of view have been submitted to vigorous discussion since the seminar invites clear statements without reservations — the atmosphere is friendly but the discussion often sharp. For the students, there is frequently the first discovery that theories are related to reality, there is a deepened understanding of their own faith positions and many times a clearer comprehension of others. Several very fine students have described the seminar as

15. General background: E. O. Galob, *Isms: A History and Evaluation;* B. E. Grimes, et al., *Values and Policy in American Society;* David Eastman, *Political System.*

Philosophical: Jacques Maritain, *Social and Political Philosophy,* ed. by Evans and Ward, and *Man and the State;* J. Messner, *Social Ethics.*

Catholic: J. S. Cronin, *Catholic Social Action,* and *Catholic Social Principles;* Martin D'Arcy, *Christian Morals, Meeting of Love and Knowledge, Mind and Heart of Love;* John C. Murray, "Contemporary Orientation of Catholic Thought on Church and State," *Theological Studies,* June 1949, and "Problem of the Religion of the State," *American Ecclesiastical Review,* May, 1951.

Jewish: Martin Buber, *Between Man and Man, I and Thou.*

Protestant: Dietrich Bonhoeffer, *Ethics;* J. Casserley, *Morals and Man in the Social Sciences;* Alexander Miller, *Renewal of Man;* Reinhold Niebuhr, *Children of Light and Children of Darkness; Self and the Dramas of History, Christian Realism and Political Problems, Interpretations of Christian Ethics, Irony of American History;* H. Richard Niebuhr, *Christ and Culture, Kingdom of God in America, Meaning of Revelation;* A. T. Rasmussen, *Christian Social Ethics;* Paul Tillich, *Love, Power and Justice,* and *New Being.*

the most mature pedagogical experience of their four-year college course.

The Institute, offering this course within the University, hopes, of course, that the students, having been made aware that there are theological implications in public policy making, will continue to develop that awareness and make contributions later to that study. Meanwhile another operation of the Institute concerned itself with men and women presently engaged in policy making in their vocational activities.

b. *The Conference*

Since its establishment the Institute has held four conferences between theologians, social scientists and representative men and women engaged in public policy making in politics, business and the church. These conferences, frankly exploratory in nature, have produced results which are worth the effort put into them and they have given the Institute valuable experience in conference method.

Participants for each conference were selected by the members of the Institute from among a roster of men and women recommended to them. The two qualities most sought for in conferees were first, a similarity of interests, and second, evidence that they were concerned about the moral and theological implications of their acts.

What is meant by the phrase "similarity of interests" can be best understood by referring to actual conferences as examples. When conferences were held with politicians, only one political party was represented at a time. It was found that by confining the representation to a single party the members felt free to speak frankly of their political problems and of their theological difficulties in relation to them. The members of a single party will admit errors in moral judgment to themselves that they would be loath to admit before the opposition. The participants at a conference of Connecticut Democratic political leaders rapidly entered into the morality of their operations; the Republicans found it difficult in the beginning to admit that they had ever done anything that was morally questionable, but once they found they could do so without fear, they freely discussed their difficulties. The business conference was confined to the representatives of the General Electric Corporation for somewhat the same reason, and the church conference to members of the Department of the National Council of Churches and the Social Education and Action Department of the Presbyterian Church, U.S.A.

All participants were provided with relevant and thought-provoking reading matter well in advance of the actual conference date. These were sent out to them with instructions that the material was intended to provide background material for the ensuing discussions as well as to raise questions in their minds. The participants, for the most part, did their "home work" well and came prepared to talk. The reading material also was given to the "faculty" (theologians and Wesleyan social scientists taking part) and they held at least one pre-conference discussion in order to select starting points for the meetings to follow and to determine some of the questions they wanted to have brought up during the talks.

Each of the conferences consisted of four meetings: one on the afternoon of the first day followed by a dinner and one in the evening of that day. The third conference met after breakfast on the morning of the second day, which was followed by a luncheon and the final conference in the afternoon. At the first meeting a faculty chairman, after providing everyone with agenda and a list of all participants, opened the discussion by presenting the broad area to be discussed and by suggesting some of the questions the "faculty" hoped would be raised. Immediately thereafter a participant, who had previously agreed to perform this function, presented a concrete problem or problems, that from his point of view held moral and theological difficulties for him, and the discussion began with this presentation. All discussions were held "off the record" unless the participants unanimously agreed to permit tape recordings. By the time the second discussion had started, a "climate" of mutual respect and trust had been established and all present felt free to speak openly and clearly about their points of view. This had important implications for people of different faith commitments because it meant that Catholics and Protestants could state their positions without being defensive or apologetic and they could listen to the positions of others without feeling that their own were being attacked. This meant that some Catholics and some Protestants learned about each other's points of view for the first time.

At the end of the conference the chairman summed up the general lines of discussion, recapitulated the problems raised, and any solutions which were suggested during the talks. Criticism and suggestions were freely made by the participants. After the conference, the "faculty" gathered and engaged in a critical review of what had occurred. The lessons learned from the conference were noted and "inwardly digested" and sometimes a summary of the whole prepared in written form.

Admittedly these conferences were very limited in scope. One thing they established rather firmly in the minds of the Institute members was a recognition that such meetings to be most productive should be several days in duration, although it was also concluded that because of the intensity of the operation it could not be prolonged much over ten days. This conclusion was thoroughly tested when some members of the Institute participated in a joint conference sponsored by the Danforth Foundation at the Harvard Graduate School of Business Administration for a period of two weeks, in the summer of 1956. Yet the week-end conference, with its limitations, is worth continuing because it is often the only one that men of affairs can spare the time to attend.

c. *The "Depth" Interview*

The Director of the Institute, Prof. Kenneth Underwood, as a result of some of the week-end conferences and the desires of some men of public position to explore the problem of theology and politics in personal conferences, engaged in some "depth" interviews on the subject. The Director, who had done a great deal of interviewing in the course of his academic studies, entered discussion with these men in an effort to understand how they conceived their role in the light of the theological convictions that they held. Attempts were made during these interviews to get the person being interviewed to try to analyze how his religious beliefs entered into the process of decision making when he was called upon to make public policy.

Interviews were held with several prominent people: a president of one of the largest life insurance companies, a senior writer for one of the large weeklies, an administrative assistant to a Senator, a Congressman and others. In all cases there was a willing participation on the part of the person interviewed, although some found it extremely difficult to verbalize their decision-making process. Some interviews were recorded, most were written up in notes taken by the interviewer at the time and immediately filled in after the interview was over. In every case, the text was typed and submitted to the person interviewed who went over it and had the final say about what was to be retained. In some cases this meant that names and places were changed to protect persons mentioned in the discussion.

Comparatively few of these interviews have been held, but the material gathered has been of great value to the Institute. Some interviews have been written up as "case studies" and those used at conferences or in the faculty-student Seminar at Wesleyan. Some of the material found its way into a book on the subject of theology and politics by some Wesleyan social scientists. All are satisfied that the technique is a valid one, within well defined limits, and efforts will be made to engage in more of this type of activity.

III. THE STUDY OF THE POLITICIAN AND HIS PROFESSION

And what has been the result of all these seminars, conferences and interviews carried out on the theory that the problem of theology and politics ought to be addressed by an inter-faith, interdisciplinary activity? The beginnings, perhaps, of a study of the politician and his profession from the standpoint of a theological inquiry. The first concrete product of this study, based partly on the findings of the Institute's seminars, conferences and interviews, and partly on the effect of these operations upon the thinking of a group of social scientists, is the book just mentioned, *The Responsibilities of the American Politician,* published under a grant from the Study Committee of the Church and Economic Life Department of the National Council of the Churches of Christ in America.

The book raises the question of the relevance of this type of inquiry and recounts the experience of the Institute in working in this field. It then focuses upon policy-making operations of the presidency, a senator, a representative in Congress, the political party, and the roles of the university and the church in relation thereto. Of these, we shall look briefly at the presidency, the Senator, and the roles of the university and the church as important parts of any study attempting to lead to a better understanding of the role of the politician and his profession.

1. THE PRESIDENCY

President Dwight D. Eisenhower is the most important single person in the United States today who is a maker of public policy. The office of the presidency itself makes this possible although the incumbents have not always seen their position in that light and at times have permitted others to be the real policy makers. There seems to be ample evidence that President Eisenhower conceives of himself in the role of a policy maker of the greatest importance despite his use of the "team" and of his deference to Congress a great deal of the time.

The personal equation is an important one in this role. A significant part of the personal equations is the theological and moral convictions[16] of President Eisenhower himself. However, these must be observed under two aspects in order to get a true picture of them. One aspect is the personal image the President has of himself as a religious and moral man as revealed in his own public and private statements and actions. In his public pronouncements the President seems to conceive of himself as a man of deep religious convictions and of great moral rectitude. His image of himself as projected in his words seems to be that he considers himself of good public morals, that his private life although generally sheltered from the public eye can be scrutinized whenever it is in the public interest to do so, and that he is a man who believes in and fears God as his Judge. He almost seems to have the old medieval

16. E.g., "Government is people, and it is just as simple as that. Get good people and you have good government. That is what I've tried to do."

conception of the king: he is a man who is under God and the law.

The public image of the President as a moral and religious man as presented by the mass communication media is that of a man who prays, attends church regularly and acknowledges his dependence upon God. It is an image of a man whose morality both public and private is worthy of emulation by all citizens. It is an image of a man who is above any unreligious or immoral action that might take place within the ranks of the administration, even when it seems as though he himself was responsible for the action in question. Thus a statement by the President that he would never appoint an Ambassador because he was a big contributor to the party was enough to remove the President from the arena of the conflict that arose over the appointment of the recent Ambassador to Ceylon.

The implications of these images are the stuff of the Institute's inquiry. How does a man who has a strong personal conception of himself as a religious and moral person, apply those conceptions to his decisions? What is the political morality of establishing the President as a man who stands above the moral issues of his own administration?

The actual formulation of policy on the part of the President, as is true of any important policy-making individual, is a blend of the personal equation and the staff process. After all the staff work is done on a serious question, it is the President himself who must finally make the decision that leads to action. It is at this point that conflicts can arise between the facts with which the researchers have to deal and the image that the decision maker has of the situation. Thus, for example, if the President takes an optimistic view of affairs this may incline him to make optimistic decisions and it may also incline staffers to suppress facts that are at variance with the President's known point of view.

The staff has a double role: At the lower echelons it finds facts and compiles them so that they can be properly used. At the higher echelons these facts must be culled and digested so that the final paper that is presented to the President is brief and couched in terms that make his decision easier. This, of course, is inescapable in any large operation. President Eisenhower has probably developed the staff process more thoroughly than any other occupant of his high office. With all the benefits that accrue from the full use of staff facilities, there is still an exceedingly important question that arises out of the relationship between a man who conceives of himself as above the vexatious difficulties that occur in that process and the men of the staff who have the presidential ear. Their view of the President's image of himself, their own image of him as a moral man, and their personal understanding of the present cultural milieu become crucial to the presidential decision-making process.

As has been said, in the end grave decisions must be made by the President and the loneliness of these decisions makes the theology and morality that informs these lonesome moments of tremendous importance.[17] It is at this point, too, that the President's image of the people, his responsibility toward them and his conception of their role in making ultimate decisions come into play. The President may be said to make his great decisions alone with God, but it is doubtful that God gives him direct inspirations at this point. Hence the great relevance of an inquiry into the whole complex process of how a President's ultimate loyalties inform the facts at his disposal upon which he must make his decisions.

2. The Role of the Senator

A Senator of the United States is a contributor to the formation of public policy by his share in the collective legislative action of the Senate. Senator John Kennedy of Massachusetts offers a good example of a Catholic politician who is aware of his policy-making function in the Senate and who has expressed his conception of this in various ways. The Senator's book, *Profiles in Courage*,[18] is an expression of admiration for statesmanship and courage of conviction of himself in the role of a statesman. His support of the Democratic party and his loyalty to the Stevenson candidacy is evidence that he is also a party politician.

As a Catholic, Senator Kennedy is in the natural law tradition;

17. Sydney Human, *The American Presidency*, Harper, 1954. Chap. 4; "The President as an Artist."
18. John F. Kennedy, *Profiles in Courage*, Harper, 1956.

he accepts that tradition and undoubtedly thinks of himself as operating within it. Yet his approach to the problems of politics evidences that he is aware of the tension which exists between the natural law tradition and the situational or relational approach to moral problems.

One of Senator Kennedy's legislative assistants[19] describes the Senator's interpretation of the politician's moral life in these terms: "He is trying to make clear to the public that he stands between expediency in the narrow sense of insensitivity to moral principle and to wider interests, and on the other hand a moral 'do-goodism' or rationalism with no adequate understanding of specific economic and political situations confronted by the politician."

Kennedy's idea of the public interest and the inevitable conflict between this and regional interests in certain matters is evidence of the Senator's attempt to be a statesman with a sense of moral responsibility to principle who must work within the political milieu of his own time and area. After painstaking research by his staff into the question of the St. Lawrence Seaway and considerable personal soul searching, Senator Kennedy decided that the Seaway was in the public interest,[20] despite the fact that the Massachusetts delegation in Congress had a strong record of opposition to the measure. His decision to vote for it was not a simple application of an abstract principle to a technical situation, nor was it an intuitional hunch applied in a crusading spirit. Rather it was a difficult decision made in the light of the Senator's own conception of his duty and responsibilities to the nation as well as Massachusetts, informed by a great deal of factual information, his acceptance of the principle of the common good, and his awareness of the possibility of severe political consequences.

Because Senator Kennedy does have a conception of his role as a moral man on the political stage, he is involved in what may be termed the politics of interpretation. He has his own conception of his role and has tried to make this clear to his constituents and his colleagues through his speeches and public statements. He seems to want people to see him as a Christian man with honest religious

19. Interview, An Administrative Assistant to Senator Kennedy, April 15, 1956.
20. See Congressional Record.

convictions who works hard in making his decisions within the factual situation as presented to him in each decision. He wants to be accepted as a good statesman and politician who is a Catholic, rather than being regarded as a Catholic who is a Senator.

There are co-religionists of his and also colleagues and fellow Democrats who are not Catholics who do not seem to want to adopt this image of the man. They would put him before the electorate as a Catholic and use him as a candidate who could swing the Catholic vote in key areas to overcome Catholic defections from the party and return the administration to the Democrats. This was the whole tenor of the Bailey[21] survey made before the nomination with its implied acceptance of the theories of bloc voting and all that those theories mean. There is some evidence in Catholic circles, too, that there are not wanting individuals who regard the Senator as a sure winner of Catholic votes without reference to much else than Mr. Kennedy's known Catholicity.

These concepts of Senator Kennedy and his role in public affairs become crucial when the question of his possible candidacy for the Presidency is considered. It does make a difference whether he is presented to the electorate as a practical statesman whose life is informed by a deep religious faith and a profound respect for the political and economic facts of life, or as a "good" Catholic who is undoubtedly "safe" on Communism and hence trustworthy in all other areas. If the Senator succeeds in establishing himself as a man of the first type, there are strong possibilities that he could become the first Catholic to attain the presidency and that he would do a good job in that office. If the Senator's friends succeed in their campaign, his election is probably doomed to become a bitter religious struggle that will recall many of the unpleasant events of the Al Smith campaign of 1928.

3. THE ROLE OF THE UNIVERSITY AND THE CHURCH

And where do the ivory towers and the sacristy fit into this pic-

21. John Bailey, Chairman, Connecticut State Central Committee of the Democratic Party. Cf. James R. Brown, "Do Catholics Vote Their Religion," *America*, August, 1956.

ture? How would the Institute conceive of them as the result of its studies and conferences?

The university has a distinct role that the book, *The Responsibilities of the American Politician,* refers to as the politics of reflection. This is a very different type of thing than the traditional role of the academician theorizing in the fastnesses of his library far removed from the realities of political life. Instead it brings the university into the political arena, but not as a pressure group nor as an intellectual elite who have all the answers at their finger tips. It is a repudiation of all that positivistic science would proclaim as the role of the learned in human affairs. Instead, it regards the university as the place where scholars, who, after personal experiences of their own in active political participation and close and intimate contact with those who are involved in politics as a life work, can study, research and reflect upon the problems that the entire community is concerned about. It is an involvement of the university, an eradication of the line between town and gown, if you will, and yet a clear realization that the university participates according to the mode of its existence. It is within the university atmosphere that those studies must be made which, addressing themselves to the problems of theology and politics, will assist greatly in leading to a profounder understanding of how society articulates itself in governmental forms and institutions. It is to this place, informed by close contact with reality yet equipped with time and facilities for reflection, that the policy maker can come, in conferences and "retreats," to gain deeper insights into his own operations and into the cultural milieu within which he must do his work. It is the belief of the Institute that this kind of interchange could lead to the production of a whole new field of knowledge about the "ways of mankind" which the traditional approaches of the social sciences, insulated from the deeper realities within the political society, can never attain.

The role of the church, then, becomes the politics of involvement. Through the renewal of contact between theology and the social sciences in the presence of the public policy makers, the Church now has an opportunity to close the gap between pulpit and pew and to enter more vigorously into the realm of public morality than it has in the past. This is something entirely different than the production of the social gospel, or the gospel of wealth, both of which were evolved by men who had no true contact either with the deeper realities of the political economy of their times or with the social sciences which would have acted as a corrective upon them. It is a lay apostolate of the present order in which the laity and clergy inform and correct each other, not in matters of doctrine which it is the clergy's mission to teach, but in the prudential means by which the informed layman can enter most effectively into the life of his community as a citizen whose Christianity informs his decisions.

For the Catholic Church in America this is a different type of involvement. In the past the American Church has tended to stress personal morality and it has not done much in the field of public morality at all. The result has been a large number of Catholics in politics, most of whom had personal lives that were satisfactory from the Church's point of view, but whose effect upon the community was sometimes adverse, to say the least. This cannot be blamed upon Protestant bigotry or opposition, but rather upon the failure of many of those Catholic politicians to see any public morality involved in their public acts. The possibilities of larger numbers of Catholic men and women entering into positions that entail public policy making — men and women who are more fully aware of the theological foundations and implications of many of their decisions, trained in an inter-disciplinary and inter-faith dialogue, and well informed as to the politico-economic facts of the situations in which those decisions are made — should be encouraged by all Catholic universities and institutions of higher learning. One way in which this stimulation can occur is through the erection and operation of similar institutes in active cooperation with non-Catholic universities and theological seminaries. It is my own conviction that such activities would be welcomed and that real contributions to learning and practical politics would result.

INDEX OF NAMES